How to Generate Great Ideas

THE SUNDAY TIMES

How to Generate Great ideas

Barrie Hawkins

KOGAN PAGE | *CREATING SUCCESS*

First published in 1999
Reprinted in 2000

Kogan Page Limited
120 Pentonville Road
London N1 9JN

The views expressed in this book are those of the author and are not
necessarily the same as those of Times Newspapers Ltd.

British Library Cataloguing in Publication Data

A CIP record for this book is available from the British Library.

ISBN 0 7494 2761 2

Typeset by Jean Cussons Typesetting, Diss, Norfolk
Printed and bound in Great Britain by Clays Ltd, St Ives plc

contents

introduction

Everything achieved by people starts with an idea. It could be an idea for a new product, or a new process, a new concept or a new marketing campaign. Maybe a new strategy for solving a problem or improving productivity, or simply a different way to organize the office.

If we improve our ability to generate ideas, then we improve our ability to do all this, and more.

Sometimes we need the 'big idea'. What is to be our big idea for that world-beating product that will take us into new markets? And to bring the big idea to fulfilment we need even more ideas! And then we need a constant flow of ideas to make and market our big idea.

change

As you read this, the world around is changing at a pace faster than ever before. How can UK businesses compete against the low-wage 'tiger' economies? And when the full might of Asian entrepreneurial spirit is finally unleashed in China, what will happen then? For years, western politicians have told us that the jobs lost from our shrinking industrial base will be absorbed by demand for service trades – but now communications technology is bringing about revolutionary means by which low-wage economies will provide many services to western countries. You – and your business or your organization if you work in one – need a never-ending flow of new ideas. New ideas for new products, new ways to attack markets, new initiatives to drive down costs, new sources of revenue, new angles on old problems, clever improvements to the design, a better use of resources, eye-catching copy, more ways to improve customer service, on and on and on.

New ideas, bright ideas, big ideas, different ideas. You may be about to surprise yourself, for you can turn out great ideas time after time, and show other people how to mine their resources, either as individuals, or as a team that will churn out ideas. Discover, then use, the tools and methods to maximize output from your mind: put in place your own production line for ideas. Post-It notes, James Bond, the Trojan horse, just-in-time, 'Happiness is a cigar called Hamlet', Direct Line insurance, the Rubik Cube, the *Guinness Book of Records*, 'The best present I have ever had!' – everything starts with an idea.

tuning in

One September morning the postman brought me a letter in a brown envelope. I recognized the sender without opening it, since in all the years I had worked for my employers they had been unable to get my name right, commonplace as it is. For some time I had been expecting to be promoted, but the letter from my employers was not a letter bringing such welcome news.

Like many people, my wife and I had often talked yearningly of starting our own business: although I did not know it then, the redundancy notice I held in my hand that morning would, in the course of time, turn a dream into reality. But a business begins with a business idea: night after night I lay awake, wondering what I could do, trying to come up with the idea for a business I could start.

When you need to come up with an idea – for whatever purpose – you don't have to do what I did, tossing and turning: since then I have made the discovery that a whole range of approaches and techniques exist that you can use to generate ideas. I have now taught these many times on my courses on ideas generation, so this book is very much based upon my experience of working with hundreds of individuals who have sought to improve their ability to generate ideas. Some of these approaches we have refined and improved, as well as inventing workable techniques of our own. This book is based upon first-hand experience of ideas.

Much of the time we will be using creative techniques to generate ideas. At this point we should pause: I know from past experience that the use of the word 'creative' may cause some readers to wonder if this is the right book for them. Over the years, on my ideas generation courses I have heard this response many times: 'But I'm not creative'. I have learned that this reaction is often caused by our association of the word 'creativity' with that which is artistic: we commonly use the word, for example, when talking about sculptors or writers. In this book when I refer to your creativity I am referring to your ability to generate ideas – and we all have the ability to generate ideas.

But a word of warning is necessary here. Many of the approaches and techniques we use are of a certain character. How best to describe that character? By the end of the book you will have your own views on that. Over the years some of the delegates I have worked with on my ideas generation courses have described many of the techniques as 'theatrical' while others call them 'American-style'. One delegate said that while practising one or two techniques he felt like a participant in a game show.

I have tried various techniques and approaches over a long period of time to improve people's ability to generate ideas: what we have here are the most effective, and by that I mean most productive of ideas. Some of these techniques may not be your cup of tea, may not appeal to your personality, especially if you are a quiet sort of person, or scholarly or analytical. But if you will try these techniques in your search for an idea – and give them a chance to do their work – you may just come up with something doing it my way, that you would not have thought of doing it your way.

Some of the things I ask you to do in your search for ideas will bring a smile to your face, some may cause you or others to laugh, one or two of the team exercises may result in uproar.

But none of these approaches are used solely to amuse you or your colleagues. Nothing I ask you to do is for entertainment purposes only: it is true that you can have a serious purpose but you do not have to have a serious face.

focusing

The starting point in your search for an idea must be: what do I want from my idea? The clearer you are in your mind about why you want to generate an idea, the more likely you are to succeed in your search for the idea that is right. The process of setting down what you want from the idea may also, by stirring your thoughts, give you some lines of thought to start with.

you

Before we look at the techniques and approaches that you can use to churn out ideas, I have a question to ask.

Over the years of teaching my ideas generation courses, I've met thousands of delegates. As you would expect, some people are not very good at producing ideas and others are quite good at generating ideas. Some people are very good at it. And a few people have a terrific ability to generate ideas. I have asked myself time and again: what makes the difference? Why is it that once we have learnt the techniques and practised them some of us are so much better at generating ideas?

My conclusion can best be explained by a real-life example. Much of my teaching has concerned helping would-be entrepreneurs generate an idea for a new business to start. On one occasion we were presenting the course in a rural part of the UK, in a small town which suffered from high unemployment, at a time when the biggest employer in the area was making everyone redundant. Two of the delegates had come to the course together: they both worked for the employer declaring the redundancies and were employed in the same part of the plant, both as storemen. They were each in their 50s and had worked for the employer for some 25 years. They had lived and been brought up in a part of the UK which has a strong, deep-rooted local culture, where families have lived for generations and where even today it is noticeable when someone moves away. These men had similar skills, similar work experience, similar environment, similar age, similar background: but one of these two people was to come up with an idea that appealed to him and that proved to work in the market-place, whereas the other will almost certainly spend the rest of his life watching daytime television.

So I asked myself, what was the difference between them? Why was one of them able to come up with a pocketful of ideas that would start a business in an economically depressed area, drawing on low capital resources, even though he had no business experience? The answer was found in their own words. The person who was so able to generate business ideas said to me: 'The job was OK. But like most people from time to time I thought about doing something else but I never got round to it. Maybe being made redundant will be a good thing, maybe this will be a chance for me to do something else, to find something I like better, to do something fresh.' His colleague, who seemed incapable of coming up with a worthwhile business idea, said: 'I'm finished. I know that. At my time of life I'm on the scrap heap.' These two people were talking about the same thing, they were both talking about the fact that they had been made redundant. The difference between them was in their *attitude* towards it, how they viewed it.

Down the years that is what I have concluded makes the difference in determining your ability to generate ideas. It is not the usual factors I would have expected: it is not education or age or resources. It is attitude.

All of us have our equilibrium upset from time to time so that we are not in the most productive frame of mind and all of us at some time or other are subject to negative influences: perhaps you received in the post this morning a letter from the credit card company, telling you that you were overdue with your payment, although you know you sent it off on time. Or maybe a colleague at work has said something to you in the last day or two which has niggled you. Or perhaps you have just been the victim of an incident of 'road rage' at the hands of some moron. Whatever, we can all of us at some time or another have our equilibrium disturbed so that we are not in a positive or up-beat frame of mind. So if at that point a work colleague comes to you and asks for your help with something and you are short with them in your response, they may wonder what is the matter with you, why are you acting that way.

But with some people a negative response, a poor frame of mind, is not an occasional occurrence. With some people it is their habitual attitude. Such individuals we can call 'negative thinkers'.

If I were to ask a friend of yours how they would describe, in general, your attitude towards life, what would be their response? Or what would be the answer of a colleague if I asked them what was your attitude generally towards your work? And if I were to ask you to look at yourself in a mirror and reflect upon your attitude, to which of the two people described above are you closer?

This book can help you improve your ability to generate ideas generally and enhance your chances of thinking up the particular idea you seek but to give it a real chance to do so you need to spring clean your mind of negative influences that may be at work while you are reading these pages. And when at any time in the future you begin work on an ideas generation session, have another sweep out of the negative factors that may be impinging on your thoughts. It is vital that you bring to the task of generating ideas a positive frame of mind. A down-beat attitude presents a block to insight and to creativity and yet the generation of ideas is a creative process.

ideas generation byword

Are you one of those individuals who can straightaway spot all the drawbacks in everything? No bad thing, you may think. But your priority when generating ideas is, if I may state the obvious, to generate ideas: evaluation must come later. And even then, bear in mind that very, very few ideas are perfect.

other people

Another important preparatory question is this: what is the attitude of those around you? What is the attitude of those persons you will be working with on the generation of ideas? And, almost certainly no less important, what is the attitude of those persons in your life who, while they do not work with you in generating ideas, their presence looms large in your life? Do you live with the sort of person who, when you tell them your great idea, will pull a face and say: 'If it's such a good idea why hasn't somebody else done it already?' That classic down-beat response makes me want to hammer on the desk. The terrible thing about it is that the better your idea, the more destructive the comment is: you think to yourself: 'Yes. If it is such a good idea why hasn't somebody else thought of it before?'

If you have heard this response from your spouse or your friend or your father-in-law when you have eagerly shared your idea with them, then of course their thinking is wrong – destructive and unnecessary. There may be 100 explanations as to why we have not heard this idea before: maybe somebody else has come up with the idea but it didn't suit their criteria or maybe they did not have the resources to carry it into fruition or maybe the timing was wrong or maybe the idea simply did not appeal to them personally or... on and on we could go. Your critic's thinking may be wrong but were you wrong to share your good idea with them? A delegate on one of my courses had been made despondent with the response of a friend with whom he had shared his good idea during an after-work drink. 'Mind you, he's always like that,' the delegate told me, 'he pours cold water on everything.' My instant response was: 'Then you should not have told him, if you knew that's what he would be like.' Mr or Ms Negative can drain you of your enthusiasm, your optimism, your initiative: such people have to be managed.

We may not choose the members of our family, but we do choose our friends. And some of us choose our colleagues: if you sit on an interview panel now, or if you do in the future, don't just consider the job applicant's skills and experience, but ask yourself: what is this person's prevailing attitude and outlook?

ideas generation byword

Whether in a formal ideas generation session with colleagues or just seeing what you can come up with together with a friend over a cup of coffee, think once, think twice, think three times before criticizing ideas suggested by others. Even if the quality of their ideas is not high, it is likely to be counter-productive if you slate the idea with a reaction such as (and I have heard this often) 'that's a stupid idea!' One of the quickest ways to improve the quality of someone else's ideas is to encourage them to practise. The more ideas they have the better the chance they will have of coming up with something worth taking further. And the more they use their mind to generate ideas the better it gets at the task – but you will discourage them from speaking up and taking part if you hack away at their confidence.

a potential ideas generation killer

While observing teams or groups of people working together to generate ideas I have, on occasions, witnessed the following.

Watching an individual, sometimes you can sense that an idea is coming to them: you can see the concentration in their face and detect their expectancy as they are about to give birth to a thought. They begin to speak – but then the words don't come out. They close their mouth again. Their eyes may narrow. What is going on here? Very likely this question has loomed in the mind of our now silent individual: 'If I say it, will somebody steal my idea?' If this could be a problem, this impediment to generating ideas with others needs to be brought out and dealt with before you start.

Frankly, if you came to me and complained that somebody else had 'stolen' your idea having heard it, I would offer you two possibilities to ponder. Perhaps the circumstances are such that you should be pleased you have been able to help this person who has stolen your idea. This was my reaction to an individual who complained that he had been generating ideas with a friend who, like him, was looking for an idea for a business he could start. The idea had worked and had taken this person off the dole after a six-month spell of unemployment following redundancy.

Second, I said to the 'victim': 'Now go away and, using your increased ability to generate ideas, having learnt and practised the techniques, generate a better idea than the one that you have forfeited. In this way you will turn what you regard as a negative outcome into a positive one. You'll be glad that you didn't stay with that old idea once you have a better one!'

clear out thinking constrictions

When I look back to my school days, I recall my teachers spending a great deal of time showing me how to retain and regurgitate facts. I remember year after year, learning how many wives a certain king had, what were their names and what happened to each of them; then being tested upon this. I remember that my teachers also spent considerable time showing me how to criticize: I remember writing lots of essays along the lines of 'Criticize Napoleon's Foreign Policy'. I do not recall my teachers devoting a great deal of time to showing me the techniques and approaches for the generation of ideas. And yet it is possible to argue that everything achieved by humankind starts with an idea.

Improve your ability to generate ideas and you benefit hugely in your life both at and outside work: you can have lots of ideas to keep the children occupied during school holidays, re-organize the kitchen, save time, improve your finances. The good news is that your ability to generate ideas can be improved dramatically and in a short space of time. We can improve our ability to come up with ideas:

- ▓ by practice;
- ▓ by knowing and applying the techniques;
- ▓ by being helped by a supportive environment.

But before I set you off generating ideas you need to clear out any 'thinking constrictions'. A thinking constriction is an impediment to creativity. Some such impediments commonly met include:

- ▓ conformity;
- ▓ fear of looking foolish;
- ▓ 'one-way' thinking;
- ▓ passivity.

conformity

Worrying about what other people may think can inhibit creativity. At a session devoted to helping businesses generate ideas for diversification I had this reaction to a seemingly profitable idea: 'If we diversify into doing that, what will people think?' The effect on the company's image can of course be a legitimate concern, but it may not be such a legitimate concern if you are worrying about your personal image and what the neighbours will think. Such a reaction can cause you to dismiss something too easily rather than taking a closer look at it. Bear in mind too that many achievements will cause you to stand out from the crowd anyway, simply because it is not what Mr or Ms Average does. Many individuals who are spectacularly successful in their own field do not strike us as conformists: this is not a term that comes to mind to describe Richard Branson or Sir Elton John or Anita Roddick.

fear of looking foolish

The ability to make others smile or laugh is a valuable asset but none of us want to unintentionally make others laugh at us: we don't want to make fools of ourselves in front of people. And yet that quite understandable fear of looking foolish could impede the flow of ideas. You and some others are working to come up with ideas to solve a problem: a thought suddenly flashes into your mind: you are about to give voice to it, you open your mouth to speak – then hesitate. 'That's a daft idea,' you think to yourself, 'they'll laugh at it'. (What you mean of course is that they will laugh at you.)

And yet, in the market-place silly-sounding ideas may appeal to some buyers. Let us suppose that 10 or 15 years ago you had been seeking an idea for a business to start. You had come to me and told me of your idea to turn up at a special occasion, such as a retirement dinner, dressed in a silly suit, perhaps a gorilla outfit, where you would sing a silly song. Looking back, I think my reaction would probably have been along the lines of: 'Hmm... interesting. But what else have you got in mind...?' Depending on your locality, my scepticism would have proved unfounded; certainly in Cambridge, a city I have known for some years, there is an established and successful kissagram service.

And bear in mind that a seemingly daft idea may be capable of being improved upon, either by you or by others. Let us suppose that in a group trying to come up with ideas, one member, Tony, has an idea which he thinks the others will laugh at, but he has read this book and he tells the others his idea. When the laughing subsides, another member of the group, Rachel, adds something to it, and then another member, Darren, having heard this, adds something more. By this time the idea is not sounding quite so daft. But we would never have come up with something which is worth considering further if Tony had not had the courage to give voice to his idea.

Incidentally, in the example just given we have seen at work one of the strong advantages of drawing together a group for the purpose of generating ideas: between them, the group may come up with an idea that would not have occurred to anybody on their own.

one-way thinking

I recently devised a new course that involves delegates in some imaginative exercises in creativity: this called for an unusual seating arrangement. I took pains to supply the venue with a diagram setting out the layout. On arrival I was very surprised to find the seating arrangement was conventional theatre-style, with neat, straight rows of chairs. I tracked down the caretaker who had set out the room for us and asked him what had happened. 'Well I looked at that piece of paper and I thought this can't be right. Anyway, there's only one way to set that room out – and that's the proper way!'

Realistically, there do exist tasks which can be undertaken by one method only, perhaps for a compelling reason such as safety, but it is too easy to allow your thinking to be influenced by automatic or lazy acceptance of the view that there is only one way of undertaking your particular task. Ask yourself and others: can't we do it some other way? If the response is 'we've always done it like that' then you may be on to something! And investigate 'we've tried it and it didn't work' – maybe the circumstances have changed since this past experiment, for example changes have occurred in the market-place.

passivity

Do not see things simply as they have always been. This is best explained by the story of the Sony Walkman, a product which could well be the biggest-selling consumer electronic product of all time. We are all familiar with the Walkman, a product which has been emulated by scores of competitors: the small box which provides portable personal listening. But think back to the days before the Walkman: are you old enough to recall the time when a tape recorder was a machine that sat on the table and used reel-to-reel tapes, themselves bigger than today's Walkman?

In those days, the late Masaru Ibuka, one of Sony's two co-founders, made it his practice to wander round the company's various research divisions to keep an eye on developments. One day in the early 1970s he found himself in the company's tape recorder research division and enquired as to progress on their current project: a tape recorder which was to be the size of a small book. He was told that engineers had difficulty in fitting speakers that would give Sony stereo quality into a machine of the desired size. 'Why not leave them out?' the company's founder suggested. The reply was that without the speakers nobody would be able to hear when the machine was played back! The co-founder of Sony pointed out that the product could be supplied with an earphone which would enable one person to listen without disturbing others.

Masaru Ibuka then enquired as to what other problems the engineers were experiencing and was told that they could not as yet fit a recording mechanism into the machine which would provide the requisite Sony quality. Back came the response: 'Well, why not leave that out as well.' This was met with incredulity. What was being proposed was a tape recorder that didn't record and which could be heard by only one person when played back. Looked at in this way the proposal was simply for a much worse tape recorder – but that assumes that a tape recorder has to record and that when it is played back everybody within earshot has to be able to hear it. Not seeing the product as it has always been enabled one individual to see something else: a different product that provided portable personal listening.

Can you learn to think like the co-founder and chairman of Sony and not see things as they have always been? You can – if you make the effort to practise switching into this mode of thinking.

your frame of mind

Your ability to generate ideas is enormously affected by your frame of mind. If you are bored, for example, you are unlikely to have inventive and valuable ideas come bubbling out of your dulled mind. By contrast, if, having dreamt of winning the lottery, you have had confirmed an all-time record win of £25 million, no doubt you will have – in your excited and energized state – ideas on how to spend it. Events not under your control, such as a win on the lottery, can affect your frame of mind; while events are, of course, not always within your control, you may nevertheless be able to some extent to at least manage those that are not. And of course you may have to manage people – such as Mr or Ms Negative.

One person you can influence is yourself. You can take steps to influence your state of mind so as to make it more productive of ideas.

visualization

Visualization is a technique that you can carry round with you, pull out and use, that is effective quickly and is free of charge. You can use the technique of visualization to create almost any desired frame of mind: you can feel in an upbeat mood, you can feel relaxed, you can feel calm. You can use it to shake off a downbeat or negative frame of mind. You can use it to motivate yourself. If you haven't used the technique before, this is what you do.

All of us create pictures in our mind. Very often this will be an automatic reaction. If I were to ask you to describe something, putting your description in writing, then, depending on how familiar you are with the item, you are highly likely, as a resource, to call up a picture of this object in your mind. For example, most of us are familiar to some extent with what an old-fashioned valve radio would look like and to make our description more effective we would almost certainly conjure up a picture in our mind of such a radio so that we could recall some of the detail. You would find yourself picturing the radio as you began drawing on your recollection.

We also create pictures in our mind when we are asleep: we call it dreaming. The pictures we create in the mind when we are asleep show just how powerful this process can be: for example, your dream can make you feel afraid, even terrified. Thus, the mind pictures you create can have a dramatic effect upon your mental state. This in turn can affect your physical state: most of us have at some time or another woken up from a nightmare, especially when we were children, with heart pounding. So the images we conjure up in our mind can affect how our body functions. Let us then use this powerful weapon for our benefit.

Like many of the techniques in *How to Generate Great Ideas*, visualization becomes more effective as you make greater use of it. So if, when the time comes, you are not particularly in the mood for generating ideas then push the button marked 'visualization' to change your frame of mind to one which is more receptive and productive.

deadlines

We all know that stress can be unhealthy, that too much pressure can cause you to work inefficiently because you find it difficult to concentrate or you become over-tired. But a modest amount of pressure can be good for you.

try this

It's Monday morning and the previous week was a difficult one. Your diary shows that at some time or another you booked a meeting for 8.45 am this morning: a session with colleagues to generate ideas for a major new project. 'I'm not in the mood for this', you think to yourself. Then try the following.

Bar the door to prevent any possible interruptions. Take off your jacket, roll up your sleeves, undo your collar, take off neck jewellery, unfasten your tie. Sit back in the most comfortable chair to hand. Close your eyes. Pretend it is that day in the future when you realize that this major new project is off the ground, that it is going to work. At that point you feel a wave of relief come over you, followed by exultation. It's time to celebrate!

So what are you going to do to mark the occasion, to reward yourself for your success? Maybe you will treat yourself to some possession you would like very much, or take that well-earned holiday, or go out for a special meal. Who will you involve in this? Who would you like to hear congratulate you? Picture the scene.

If you make the effort with visualization and practice, you will find these scenes very real. You are there. You can *see* the expressions on people's faces. You can *hear* the sounds: perhaps you can hear someone saying, 'Well done! I didn't think you'd do it, but you have. So, well done!' You will be able to *smell* the aroma of the delicious meal that is being cooked for you. You will be able to hear the chink of glasses as friends and colleagues drink a toast. You will be able to *feel* the champagne bubbles tickle your nose. Savour this scene for one minute.

Then come back to today. Now isn't that a much better frame of mind in which to start your ideas generation session?

You can impose a little bit of pressure on yourself by drawing up and sticking to deadlines. Having a deadline to work to can help motivate you to get on with the task in hand and prompt you into faster thinking. It can increase your sense of purpose. So if you need ideas for that new project, then set a deadline: fix the date for a short-list of ideas and set a second date for the completion of evaluation procedures and making known the idea that has worked its way to the top of the list.

The problem with setting deadlines that only you know about is that only you will know if you break them, so tell the world: announce to everyone the date of your deadline. Do not just tell those people who are involved in the project or will be affected by it, but choose to tell others as well: especially tell Mr or Ms Negative, who knows that you are not going to get it done. What an incentive you will have to get on with it! You won't want to lose face, especially in front of Mr or Ms Negative.

get away

Our immediate environment affects us much more than we often realize. Contrast, for example, your behaviour when visiting a peaceful country churchyard with your behaviour when joining the crowds thronging a carnival. In the quiet of the churchyard you are conscious of every sound and instinctively lower your voice, while the carnival is conducive to laughter and calling out, even rushing about if you are young or fit! Recall how it feels to 'get away' from the work-place after a wearing day and unwind in your home environment.

You can employ this effect to your advantage when generating ideas. If you are not 'in the mood' or the session has stalled or thinking has become stale, move to a different place. Even changing rooms can be effective, such as moving from the more relaxed environs of your sitting room to the brighter kitchen with its busier look and feel. Or adjourn from the office to the local pub or, weather permitting, to the local park.

You will find such a move may also affect the quality and type of ideas you generate: getting up and moving somewhere else can be of benefit well beyond the effort involved.

stop thinking about it

This technique is so simple and obvious that we often overlook using it to help us.

The ideas generation has come to a halt. You sit there sucking your pen, looking at a blank sheet of paper. Writers call it 'writers' block'; you might say you have a mind block. Or maybe what you are looking for is 'on the tip of your tongue' but you just can't frame the thought or bring out the answer.

If you've ever done crossword puzzles, you'll know how you can give up, go to bed and wake in the morning with the word you were looking for in your head. Sleep has given your subconscious time to work and this is the process you are making room for if you call a halt to thinking about the problem. When an ideas generation session becomes bogged down, try just leaving it. Go away and do something else, but it needs to be a something else which fully occupies your thoughts and attention, allowing your subconscious time to sift and sort the information in your mind. You will come back to the session refreshed, often with a new track to follow – and sometimes with the solution that was actually staring you in the face but you were too busy thinking to see!

play with the environment

We have seen that a change *of* environment can be a useful move to make. You can benefit also from making changes to the environment.

We either generate ideas on our own or by working with someone else: we have noted that our own mood – and other people's mood – is, naturally, drastically affected by the surrounding environment. Colour, lighting, music, and scent all play a big role in affecting the ambience of the room, helping to influence the mood of each of the persons gathered; in turn the mood of each individual affects the other people present.

Making changes to the room in which you or the group are working can affect not only the number of ideas generated but also the nature of those ideas.

On some ideas generation sessions I have divided the session into two halves. In the first half I ask the participants to create the sort of working environment you would find, for example, in a well-functioning office. If you have enough participants you can divide them up into small groups, all working in the same room but at separate tables and in this way you can create that 'hum' found in a busy office environment. This half of the session is likely to produce more practical, realistic ideas.

For the second half of the session I invite the participants to be more relaxed, to consciously enjoy the session, and I produce some aids to help create this lighter atmosphere. It is here that I turn on the music. Whatever the choice of music it is likely to result in a complaint from at least one participant that it is not to his or her taste. Most classical music doesn't lend itself to creating a light atmosphere, although a collection of snatches of well-known works that sound triumphal has made a useful final tape to round off the session. The swing of Glenn Miller's Big Band sound goes down well with most participants over the age of 20, and nearly everybody recognizes the tune 'In The Mood', which makes an apt piece of music to open an ideas session.

Some experts in creativity say that our most creative period is when we are small children, since which time our teachers and parents have devoted themselves to restricting our creativity by imposing rules, discipline, codes of conduct and conformity. On the basis that this may be right, I have on occasion used background music that most people associate with their childhood. Tunes from Disney such as 'Whistle While You Work' and 'Heigh-Ho, Heigh-Ho, It's Off To Work We Go' may benefit from their association with genius. This second half of the session produces the more crazy and inventive ideas.

I always say to participants: 'We want to hear your daft ideas.' The expression on the faces of some people indicates they are beginning to think they are perhaps wasting their time, that they have not come along to produce daft ideas but, as we have noted, silly-sounding ideas may work in the market-place and can perhaps be improved upon. Having made those points I then get out the balloons. If you are leading such a session you may prefer to start with the music and bring in the balloons later to inject something new into the proceedings.

How far you go with changes to the environment to lighten the mood will depend upon your personality, your boss (if you have one), and the culture of the organization in which you are working. In this half of the session I usually try to create a party atmosphere. Of course the more like a wild party it all gets, the crazier the ideas and the greater the likelihood that there will be a lot of chucking out to do later. But laughter can be a release mechanism and thus a spur to inventiveness.

push out negative influences

The technique of visualization we looked at earlier in this chapter can help put you into a more productive frame of mind. If you feel you are not set up for generating ideas, to help alleviate a serious ailment it may be that a medicine other than visualization is required. It may be a worse case than simply not being in the mood for generating ideas: it could be the case that you have something troubling you, there is something on your mind.

All of us at some time have our equilibrium upset by events or other people. So perhaps at the start of the session you have booked with colleagues to come up with ideas to solve that 'big problem', your equilibrium has been upset by some incident that keeps coming back into your mind. You are trying to forget what your teenage son has done – although you can't believe that he could do something so stupid!

At the commencement of each session I have held with people to generate ideas I asked them to leave behind their negative thoughts. If you are going to produce ideas you need to approach your task in a constructive, up-beat, optimistic frame of mind. If you are to give yourself the fullest chance to come up with workable ideas you must resolve to push out negative thoughts which impinge upon your mind.

try this

Now, if I ask you to do that, to commence your ideas generation session with a mind freshly spring-cleaned of negative thoughts I am sure you will resolve to do so. However, research shows that you are much more likely to carry out a mental resolve if you accompany your mental resolution with a physical act.

Buy some grey paper. At the start of your ideas generation session write these two words on this boring piece of paper: 'negative influences'. Write the two words in some way of your choosing which gives emphasis to them. Perhaps you will write the two words over and over again on the sheet of paper, or perhaps you will underline them 30 times, or perhaps you will write them in red, or perhaps you will write them in huge block capitals.

What we are about to do next is even more effective in a group session than when you are working on your own, because you will be encouraged by the participation of the others – so be aware of that and concentrate hard on this exercise when doing it alone.

Ask all those present to stand. Produce a waste paper bin and place it where everybody can see it. Move out of the line of fire and invite the participants to attack the piece of grey paper. You can take out your frustration with the event – or person – that has upset your equilibrium on that piece of grey paper. Yell loudly at it and screw it into a ball, then hurl it into the waste paper bin.

When I am leading an ideas generation session and using this technique I use moral blackmail on the participants. You can tell them that how well they undertake this task is a useful barometer of how well the session is likely to go: a foretaste of the extent to which they will throw themselves into the session. If you have enough people you should find the noise is such that other people in the building come down to investigate what is going on. I think one person should be enough to produce this result.

brainstorming: setting up

If you haven't met the term before, brainstorming is the coming together of a group of people for the purpose of generating ideas. Some people apply the expression to an individual working alone trying to come up with ideas, but for me brainstorming is the process whereby ideas are born of the interaction of a group of people.

People coming together for the purpose of generating ideas – what luxury! Everything in the world achieved by humankind begins with an idea, yet we devote so little time to the generation of new ideas. Instead, we allow ourselves to become preoccupied with the daily grind. Regular brainstorming sessions will quicken your thinking, enhance your ability to spot opportunities, make you more daring in your thinking, take you deeper in your thinking, pull you into exploring new channels.

Brainstorming is the coming together of a group of people for the *sole purpose* of generating ideas. You haven't come together to discuss the government or last night's match!

who will be in your gang?

My experience of working in hundreds of brainstorming
sessions is that if we generate 100 ideas, probably 98 of them
will be discarded. Now if that statistic makes you sink back in
your chair, let me say that to generate 100 ideas is no big deal.
My observations and subsequent analysis of a random sample
of brainstorming sessions I have convened shows that if I have
a group of motivated people who are properly briefed, for
every 52 ideas they generate we would have at least one worth
taking beyond the initial sifting of the ideas generated.

Naturally, numerous variable factors will affect this, such as
the levels of intelligence and education of the individuals who
make up the brainstorming group. Also, the effectiveness of the
group will be much affected by the personalities of the individuals in the group and their inter-relationship. If you have
control or influence over who makes up the group, it is open to
you to construct a group made up of personalities who you feel
will together be the most effective: a great deal of research has
been carried out on team building and there are absorbing texts
on the subject that go into detail outside the scope of this book.

Sometimes who is in the group will be dictated by circumstances (or your boss) and so you end up with a representative
from marketing, somebody from finance, a member of the sales
team, and the section manager, whether or not personality tests
would indicate these individuals could make an effective team.
If this is your situation then take comfort: carefully constructed
teams do not always bring it off. In creating an artwork or
cooking or product development you can put together all the
winning ingredients and still produce a dud. What could be less
predictable than how a group of individuals will react together
on one particular occasion, the day after one of them has
received bad news, a time when another is pondering whether
he has a future with this organization at all, and a third feels he
is sickening for a cold?

special roles

That said, even if I am not in a position to select the members of the brainstorming group, I put together a questionnaire, which I ask potential participants to complete, the purpose being to indicate who is likely to be suited for one of two major roles in the group. I am looking for an 'organizer' and a 'mover'. Leave a group totally to its own devices and occasionally it can either come to a halt because it has 'got stuck', or it has fallen into evaluating ideas rather than generating them.

organizer

I am reluctant to label the organizer 'team leader', even though some of their functions may be those you would expect of a leader: the term works against the others seeing themselves as equals, both able and required to make an equal contribution. The organizer needs to be both an organizer and a decision-taker. He or she also needs an air of authority: they will have to pull up the team member who hasn't come to terms with the rules and disrupts the flow of ideas with criticisms and comments.

The team will also need a scribe to record the ideas as they are generated: someone who can write quickly and legibly and who can spell, otherwise they waste time agonizing over how to spell a word, feeling pressurized because their spelling is on display. The holder of this office can be a volunteer but if the team cannot quickly agree on this then the organizer will have to appoint the scribe: an example of why the organizer needs an air of authority. An ability to marshal the others may also be required of the organizer in order to get them back after coffee. At brainstorming sessions I convene, I present the team organizer with a special badge with their official title printed in blood red as a symbol of their raw power.

The organizer may need to have a voice that can be heard when others are speaking and the ability also to stand up and address the group.

movers

Identification of the 'leader' among the group can lead too often to Mr or Ms Evaluation being put in charge of the team. In my experience what is most effective is undoubtedly to identify the person I call the 'mover'. We need to identify the natural creative thinker.

Although I do not ask our mover to take control of the team, their task is to interrupt negative or unproductive discussion – and they will need the confidence to do this. I have found that as long as a team contains one creative person whose instinct is not to evaluate, that team can function.

Give the mover this instruction: 'move the team along'. We are looking for the type of person who is not afraid to throw in a 'wacky' idea to allow the team to change tack if they are stuck. But, rather than confront the person who wants to deliberate and evaluate, we want a mover who will keep the team working, keep the ideas flowing and prevent stagnation.

Set the other members of the group a task and take the movers aside: put them in the picture as to their special role. Present each mover with a special badge: a yellow badge is apt as it symbolizes brightness and get-up-and-go.

who is suited for what role?

It may be that the personalities of the members of the group are sufficiently well known to you that you feel confident in deciding who would make an organizer and who a mover. If not, you will need a simple questionnaire. A time-efficient method for devising a straightforward questionnaire is to list a number of statements and ask each member of the group to tick those statements which they consider apply to them. Instruct them that there are no right or wrong answers and that they may find they have ticked all the statements or that they have ticked none. Limit the time allowed for the completion of the questionnaire and instruct them not to agonize over their answers: almost certainly their initial reaction is the correct one. As a minimum, I ask participants to tick whichever of the following they feel applies to them:

1. I feel comfortable joining in small group discussions.
2. I get a kick out of helping others.
3. Some people would describe me as non-conformist.
4. I like to try new ways of doing things.
5. I am good at quickly spotting the drawbacks in something.

You may be able to have your questionnaire circulated and returned in advance, in which case you can construct a more searching and complex form, but if participants have to complete it on the day, beware, for your sake, of making it too lengthy. Unless you have huge numbers to handle, sifting through five answers on each questionnaire can be done quickly while the members of the group are set a task to occupy them. (That task can be collecting the materials they will use in their brainstorming teams, about which more later.)

When checking the questionnaires, immediately look to statement five: if a participant has ticked this I immediately disqualify them from the roles of organizer or mover. In either role the individual will have a higher profile than other team members and more chance to hold the floor: a strong tendency to evaluate is not a quality desirable in the holders of these positions. A tick for statement number one hopefully indicates that this person is likely to participate: a prerequisite for both the organizer and the mover.

Depending on the circumstances, it may be that one member of the group will benefit more than the others from a successful outcome to an ideas generation session. Indeed, it may be that the exercise is for the sole benefit or interests of one particular individual in the group. Perhaps, for example, the family has come together to generate ideas for what John can do when his notice of redundancy expires, or perhaps all the departmental heads have got together to help solve a problem that primarily affects one department. Or maybe the situation is that only some members of the group will benefit from a successful outcome or that there will be considerable variations in the extent to which those present will benefit.

If not everybody will benefit to the same extent you may need to crank up the motivation of individuals (about which more later) but accepting that some people will put more effort into it than others, an affirmative answer to question two should help produce an organizer or mover prepared to participate.

Statement three is there to elicit candidates for mover: such an individual is more likely to provide the spark that keeps the team moving. Identifying likely candidates as mover is also the prime function of statement four. To sum up:

- ■ those who tick 1 and/or 2 should be fine as a mover or organizer;
- ■ those who tick 3 and/or 4 should be OK as a mover;
- ■ a tick for 5, in my experience, eliminates that participant from either office.

break them down

If you have sufficient numbers it can be extremely effective to split your group into teams. A group of 10 or 12 (or more) provides the conditions which encourage the less confident individuals not to participate fully. Not only may having a smaller audience to address encourage the more timid individual, it also makes it easier for the team organizer to spot who is sitting further back and relaxing, and then encourage their involvement.

Dividing your group into teams for at least part of the session also permits the introduction of that competitive spirit which can give such a boost to performance. My experience is that, sufficient numbers permitting, splitting the group convened for a brainstorming session into two or more teams can be the single most effective device open to you. To build the most competitive atmosphere requires the services of a master of ceremonies (MC) who is not a member of any team and can lead what is becoming an event. For the purposes of the remainder of this book I appoint the reader MC for your brainstorming session.

How many in a team? One is an individual, two is a pair, three is a tiny team, four is a number usually capable of creating a hum. If your teams are working at tables, since most tables have four sides a team of three tends to look as if it has one member missing. A team of seven seems to be the number at which it starts to become easier for one member to participate less than the others without it being obvious.

pick and mix

You are likely to get a broader range of experience if brainstorming teams comprise both sexes. If you have sufficient people to give you a number of teams, beware of a team forming from the 'lads at the back of the class'. The message that you can have a serious purpose without having a serious face may be misinterpreted by an all-male team of younger men. Young male executives on a Friday afternoon, after a lunchtime drink in the pub, may unwind as they run up to the weekend, and mucking about may substitute for work.

If some of the people gathered know one another it may be more effective to split them: this is an opportunity for them to interact with people they do not normally get the chance to work with, to benefit from input based upon other's experience.

breaking the ice

How well do the members of your brainstorming group or team know one another? It may that they only meet occasionally, for example they come into contact every so often through managers' meetings. Possibly some members of the team have not met the others before, for example someone who has only recently joined the company. As a rule of thumb I would suggest that unless all the members of the team are friends or they work together virtually every day, you will need to help glue them together.

On one occasion a company in the insurance industry decided to tap into its agents for ideas to improve its range of insurance products, holding ideas generation sessions in each sales region. One particular region had over 20 agents, some of whom were only on nodding acquaintance and two of whom, as recent recruits, had not previously met all the other agents in their region. If you have a similar situation you will need, as we did, an ice-breaker.

Before putting them into brainstorming teams I have everybody working together with a partner for a few minutes. Of course, this will go more smoothly if they get on with their partner. In my experience, in the case of someone you don't know, you are more likely to get on with that person in the first few minutes if you share similar tastes and interests. How can we discover the tastes of persons we do not yet know?

Perhaps the most common ice-breaker used to relax such a group of strangers is where the chairperson suggests the attendees turn to the person next to them: they each introduce themselves and then have a little chat.

I recall vividly attending as a delegate a seminar where the seminar leader employed this ice-breaker. I turned to the delegate sitting in the next seat: he was a gentleman of distinguished appearance, seemingly in his 60s, with silver hair, half-moon spectacles, three-piece severe pinstripe suit and tie with a coat of arms. The enrolment instructions had told us we could attend wearing clothes in which we felt comfortable: I felt comfortable in one of my old, familiar jumpers. As this gentleman weighed me up, I noticed that my old, familiar jumper had a hole in the sleeve which had previously escaped my attention. As the half-moon spectacles moved slowly up and down, taking in all the detail of the gentleman's potential partner, the hole in my sleeve grew bigger and bigger. As I became increasingly tense, the thought occurred to me that this exercise was designed to relax me. Seemingly I did not share my proposed partner's tastes or judgement as to what was suitable apparel in which to attend a business course.

A useful clue to your tastes and your personality is what you are wearing. At brainstorming sessions at which it is necessary to break the ice, I invite the participants to wander round the room and mingle until they spot somebody who is dressed something like them. Colour can be extremely useful here, as can type of footwear and style of spectacles.

So if you are in the chair at a session to generate ideas for that new product or to improve customer service or to come up with a solution to the 'big problem', and you need an ice-breaker, invite those present to wander about the room and find someone who is dressed somewhat like them or is wearing the same colour. The blues and greys of business suits can have a limiting effect here, but women tend to employ a bigger range of colours and today most males are willing to inject a bit of colour – and even some humour – into their business wardrobe by their choice of tie. I suggest that the guy with the yellow tie seeks out the woman with the yellow blouse: a colour perhaps likely to appeal to more lively individuals, those who are good at getting going in the morning.

You may well be thinking that all this will unravel if Mike is wearing that tie only because his parents-in-law bought it for him for Christmas and they are staying with him at the moment… it's a possibility, but as a general rule, this ice-breaker works. I used this once at a meeting of sales representatives gathered together from throughout the UK: two previously unacquainted attendees who partnered up using this method subsequently married and I received an invitation to the wedding. So beware of its effectiveness.

contact

If it is necessary for you to prime the motivation and interest of some of the participants, when the brainstorming team is drawn together request that each member shakes hands with every other member of the team. Lots of research shows that we are much more likely to participate and care about each other if we have had some physical contact with the people we are working with: so we want the participants to touch each other. We don't want any funny business, of course: contact can be achieved by gripping the other person's hand firmly and looking them in the eye while shaking hands. We want something more energetic, and carrying more of a message, than the polite reticent handshake still common among the educated classes of English society. And if it is necessary to break the ice by partnering up participants before they get into teams, they should also greet their partner in this fashion.

When I act as MC for brainstorming teams where the members are not all well known to one another, I ask a participant to step forward. I demonstrate with him or her how the swinging arms come together in a firm clasp of hands, the face lights up with a smile and our eyes meet.

tools

The brainstorming team needs a pen and some paper. Do not use the usual A4 sheets of paper. I believe people's creativity will be enhanced if we do what we can to mark out this coming together to generate ideas as something not part of the ordinary daily chores, a time for us to free up our creativity, to use our minds, to explore in our minds, to see how deep we can dig and what we can bring out that is different and exciting and worthwhile and valuable. So try making the brainstorming sessions that you lead larger than daily life. Big sheets of paper are easy to obtain: you can use flip-chart paper. Purchase some big, fat felt-tipped pens in bright colours.

Instruct whoever gives out the equipment to the teams that they must inject some energy into their work: we don't want young Darren ambling round the room looking as if he is not part of the proceedings and disinterested. Tell Darren to scurry between the teams and to make sure once the teams start brainstorming that they don't run out of paper: indeed, a small way in which you can exert pressure on the team is a regular delivery of more sheets so that the paper waiting to be covered with ideas is piling up. Accompany each delivery of paper with an announcement, in a loud voice: 'More paper!' Borrow or buy a large clock and site it prominently.

space

The physical layout of the room in which the brainstorming takes place has a role to play in creating the beneficial competitive environment between the teams. To encourage a team spirit, each team needs to view itself as an entity. That this is so can be physically reinforced by a seating arrangement in which each team works in a little island of its own, separated by channels wide enough to allow the MC to run from team to team in safety. Allow sufficient space between teams so that no team is distracted by the voices of members of another team, nor can they listen in to a competing team and steal their ideas.

brainstorming: setting off

Practice and motivation will increase the quality of brainstorming sessions but they can come apart unless *fundamental rules* are strictly adhered to. In my experience the three rules you must lay down are.

no negative comments

The members of the group are not there to complain: if the coffee was cold tell somebody about it during a break. We want to create an atmosphere that is upbeat: creative, constructive, positive, optimistic, and supportive. So if a member of your group throws in a good idea, praise him or her. A constructive attitude will lead you to build upon the ideas of others, to enhance them. An optimistic frame of mind will cause you to reach out for new ideas, exciting ideas, the biggest number of ideas ever, help create a buzz in which everyone thinks it's working and taking off and we *are* going to come up with something better and this is great!

no evaluation

This is the most difficult rule of all to enforce. It is a natural reaction to want to give an evaluation of somebody's idea when hearing it, especially if you have some experience as to the viability of that idea. It's difficult not to respond: 'It's the wrong time of year for that', or 'That will never work in Asia', or 'We did almost the same thing years ago and it was a total flop.'

Your purpose for now in the brainstorming session must be to generate ideas: evaluation comes later. If you are new to brainstorming you may pull a face at this stage. Your reaction may be: what is the point of generating ideas if we don't evaluate them? But I am not suggesting that you are banned from evaluating, merely that you are banned from evaluating ideas during the brainstorming session itself.

Generating and evaluating ideas at the same time is like trying to put your foot on both the brake and the accelerator together: the two are incompatible. An individual may feel dispirited when his or her idea is pulled apart, no matter how tactfully it is done – hardly the frame of mind for churning out further ideas. As idea after idea is tossed aside in the process of evaluation, the group as a whole can become demoralized.

The task for now is to generate ideas. The trick is to generate *enough* ideas. The more ideas you generate, the better the chances are that somewhere in there will be what you are looking for.

keep up the momentum

If the brainstorming team is stuck: move on! Do not become despondent and do not allow the team members to look at one another wondering what they can say now. A lively mover in the team – likely to be a lively personality as a rule – draws on tools and techniques from this book. Once you have a handful of ideas on paper you can keep the ideas coming: you can brainstorm ideas about ideas. Don't let the team sit in a rut. As soon as you sense an uncomfortable silence, bring out this next technique.

generate ideas about ideas

Select one of the ideas already generated and generate ideas about that.

Often the ideas thrown out early on will be very broad in nature and have possibilities for development. For example, in a brainstorming session seeking ideas for new products that the company could develop, one team member suggested 'version for disabled people'. Returning to this minutes later, the huge number of possible versions to be explored was immediately obvious because of the diversity of disabilities people suffer.

In the earliest minutes of the same brainstorming session I saw 'children's version' recorded and 'novelty version' suggested: again, such ideas are starting points for a burst of further ideas.

This process of generating ideas about ideas can be repeated throughout the session, it is self-perpetuating. Thus the list of ideas for novelty versions included 'Disney version', itself a starting point for further ideas.

As a writer I hear talk from some other writers about the dreaded 'writer's block', that situation where the writer has dried up and the pen no longer moves across the paper. To me, this is a self-inflicted state. There are billions of people on our planet, there are billions of things happening, we have millions of years of history, we have the future – how can there be nothing to write about? So too with your brainstorming team: there is always something around from which you can generate ideas.

topics

Allow the team members to set off just flinging down whatever ideas come to them: this gives you the best chance of producing quickly that list of initial ideas which they can then use to generate ideas about ideas. So allow and encourage them to generate the broadest sort of ideas possible at the start.

Once initial ideas start to run out, the team can then use 'topics'. This is where the team generates ideas based upon a single source or objective. For example, in a brainstorming session I led on generating ideas for improvements to that commonplace product the shopping trolley (not to be confused with the supermarket trolley) topics suggested included:

- what would I have to do to export it successfully to the Middle East?
- what would I have to do to export it successfully to the United States?
- a child's version;
- a version for BMW drivers (the popular image of the shopping trolley conjures up a vision of a plastic tartan box on wheels trundled along by a pensioner wearing a hairnet, so this would be a tough market for the product to crack);
- a dual-purpose version;
- making a fashion statement;
- using it on different terrain (eg not pavements);
- make a miniature version;
- sell it in Harrods;
- make it usable in Scandinavian winter conditions;
- a multi-purpose version.

These topics are starting points for generating clusters of ideas around them.

Depending on how experienced your people are in brainstorming, you may wish to help keep things moving by coming up with a list of topics *before* setting off the brainstormers. This can be written up on a flip-chart for everybody to see or, alternatively, each team can have its own list. You may choose to prepare this list yourself beforehand if your brainstormers are very inexperienced and lacking in confidence. Or you could ask the group as a whole to suggest these starting points. A third alternative is for each team to draw up its own list.

inspiration list

A possible advantage with alternatives two and three is that an individual or a team may be better motivated to come up with ideas for their own topics. I've had it said to me: 'We found it hard to come up with ideas for the topic you suggested.' It is an easy excuse for a brainstormer that he or she hasn't been given good material to work with.

To me, the essential characteristics of successful ideas generation are: *momentum* and *delving deeper*.

But we have to get in motion, we have to start off. So maybe we need help even in generating our list of topics. In which case I have an 'inspiration list' I use over and over again:

- ■ people;
- ■ places;
- ■ concepts;
- ■ events;
- ■ history.

What we are doing here is using starting points to come up with starting points. Add to it some of your own.

the warm-up

If not everybody in your group is familiar with brainstorming, have a practice run to give them a better idea of what is being asked of them beforehand. The warm-up exercise often used by groups coming together to brainstorm ideas for new products, the Uses Brainstorm, works as a good general warm-up.

Here we take an item and think of as many ideas as we possibly can for the beneficial use of this product. Tell the brainstormers that this is what is required of them but don't tell them yet what the particular item is. While the big pens and giant sheets of paper are being given out leave them wondering what the item is they are going to have to brainstorm ideas around: this may help to give a little edge to the proceedings.

A useful item for this exercise, and one I frequently use, is the common brick. Impose a time limit – five minutes should suffice – in which the brainstormers have to come up with as many ideas as they possibly can for the beneficial use of a single brick.

The exercise may not at first sight seem particularly challenging, since this is an object we are all familiar with – we are not being asked to generate ideas for an unfamiliar item whose uses may not be known to us. But using a brick for the exercise gives it this twist: while we are familiar with the uses to which bricks are put, eg to build a wall or a house or a garage, these are uses for bricks plural. We can all immediately suggest ideas for the use of a pile of bricks, but what are we going to do with a single brick? Don't forget to make use of topics. Topics for the brick exercise can include:

- ▧ the garden;
- ▧ on holiday;
- ▧ art;
- ▧ kids;
- ▧ Christmas;
- ▧ the office;
- ▧ granny;
- ▧ health;
- ▧ in battle;
- ▧ hobbies.

Having used this warm-up exercise now with hundreds of brainstorming teams, I can report that a team of between four and six members will, in five minutes, come up with an average of 38 uses. Around 60 ideas is a high-performing mark achieved by about one team in eight and an exceptional team can achieve 80 ideas. The record I have witnessed is 114 (on the other hand, I have also worked with teams who have scored 13, 14 or 15, the record being a team of five who scored 10 ideas generated in five minutes).

The brick exercise is a useful indicator of the extent to which individuals or teams need to loosen up their thinking. It is not simply that we have to overcome being unused to dealing with this item as a single entity: the list of uses the brainstormers come up with will tell you whether or not they are making the leap in their thinking and not seeing the brick as a brick.

Early in the process, most people will think about possible uses in the home, a familiar environment, and a frequent suggestion is to use the brick as a bookend. But one bookend is of limited use; however, if we break the brick in half, it can of course be used as a *pair* of bookends. The brainstormer who suggests a pair of bookends no longer sees the brick as a single item. They no longer see the brick as it appears on the table before them.

Special praise went to the member of a team who came up with juggling as a beneficial use of a single brick. As she explained, 'If I throw the brick up in the air enough times I am bound to drop it and break it in two, in which case I'll have two halves of brick to juggle with. This will be more difficult than juggling with one brick so I am likely to drop one of these even sooner than I dropped the single brick and if one of these halves breaks in two, then I will have a juggling set of three brick portions. So a beneficial use for a single brick is as a juggling set.' Break up the brick into fragments and as rubble we open up a whole new range of uses.

Taking this line of thinking even further, we can grind down the brick and produce brick dust, thus opening up yet another line of possibilities. If you are attacked by a mugger, for example, you can throw it in the mugger's face to ward him off.

a little bit of pressure

Imposing a strict time limit is an example of the use of deadlines to get people moving, a technique we looked at in Chapter 4. You can enhance this effect by using the countdown technique. During the warm-up brainstorm instruct delegates when they have only one minute remaining. Brainstorms later in the session, or in subsequent sessions, can be of variable length and with longer time limits; for these the countdown can be announced in stages. So for example in a 20-minute brainstorming session I announce when participants are half-way through, then when they have five minutes remaining, then two minutes, then one minute, and finally 10 seconds to go.

You can physically inject energy and pace into the proceedings by running from team to team to tell them individually how much time they have remaining. The moment of glory is of course when the team announces what proves to be the highest number of ideas achieved by any team. This competitive element can be heated up by the MC during the brainstorming: half-way through inform the lower-scoring team of the number of ideas their higher-scoring rivals have achieved.

props

Once a team has generated their initial burst of ideas, you can help prevent them flagging by handing them a prop which will act as a prompt. For example, and most obviously, during a session on ideas to improve a product, give them an example of the product. As we want the teams during their warm-up brick exercise to achieve an encouraging score, don't overlook giving each team at some point or other a brick to examine. Encourage each team member to handle the brick. Feeling its texture or the indentation on the top may suggest ideas.

If a team is working on a product, ask them to consider dismantling it.

prizes

We all know that the more motivated we are the better we perform and that rewards can play a big role in motivation. So make generous use of prizes to reward the team which achieves the greatest number of ideas against the clock. Award further prizes for the team that comes up with an idea or specified number of ideas that the MC or a judge considers to have special merit; these could be the most original ideas, or the most saleable, or whatever, according to your needs.

I have tried out a variety of prizes at brainstorming sessions and settled on a single item some years ago for all my prizes. For the warm-up session I announce to the team members just before setting them off that the organizer of the highest-scoring team will step forward on behalf of the team to receive a prize against a background of rapturous applause.

In keeping with the philosophy that you do not have to have a serious face to have a serious purpose, a little bit of theatre has always gone down well here. At this point I stride off to fetch a large gleaming red metal cashbox which I unlock before the participants to reveal my stock of prizes: a treasure chest of lollipops. Trivial as this prize may strike you, I can assure you that the longer our ideas generation session goes on the more prized these lollipops become. At the end of a day devoted to the competitive generation of ideas, emotions can be aroused and heated exchanges take place as to the correctness or otherwise of a particular decision to award a prize. At an in-house session devoted to generating ideas for re-organizing the sales force, drawing on the talents of the company's 15 sales managers, one team went on strike and refused to continue to participate when they felt cheated out of a rightful lollipop!

Success in the warm-up exercise results in the awarding of a single lollipop to the team organizer. In consequence, the other members of the team will benefit only if their organizer is generous in spirit and passes the lollipop round for each member of the team to enjoy a lick. The stakes can be upped from this by offering as the prize at a subsequent brainstorm a lollipop for *each member* of the team!

A final Grand Brainstorm can climax in the awarding of a giant lollipop of the sort usually retailed at seaside rock emporia. I usually keep a stock of these, the need to stock up giving me an excuse to visit twice annually the remarkable sandstone cliffs at Hunstanton on the delightful Norfolk coast.

In the serious event of a non-availability of the ordinary lollipops at your local sweet shop, I have found Sherbet Dabs serve as an acceptable alternative, seemingly going down exceedingly well with a group of redundant executives participating in a job-seeking ideas session.

team identification

How much effort you put into cultivating the competitive spirit between the brainstorming teams must depend on whether this is a one-off ideas generation session or whether the participants will be coming together in the future.

To boost the competitive spirit between the teams, give a boost to the members of each team seeing their team as an entity. This can be helped by giving them team names. It is in any case more efficient than the MC having to say 'and the team on my left having scored 99, let's hear now from the team by the coat-rack.' The MC could dish out boring identity labels such as Team A, Team B, etc but this is hardly in keeping with the inventive character of an ideas generation session. Ask the members of each team to think of a name: this can itself be a team ice-breaker and a small warm-up exercise. If time is short ask them to give over a few minutes of their coffee-break chat to suggesting names.

The identification process can be aided by having the team organizer write the team name on a (preferably prepared and coloured) sheet of paper which can be folded so as to be displayed on the team table. Ask each team organizer to stand and announce the chosen team name to the whole group. If this is an in-house session then inspiration can be derived from the company or organization; otherwise, the team members can be given freedom of choice. If the session is related to business, the team members may wish to dedicate themselves to a successful entrepreneur: recently among the teams in one group – drawn from the PR industry – I had the Virgin Soldiers, Anita's Army, and Sugar's Shooters. Some teams march under the banner of a business guru: so I have worked with Tom's Team and Sir Trouble-shooter's Team. It so happens that all of these teams have performed well, so for the inspiration they didn't know they had given, thanks to, respectively, Richard Branson, Anita Roddick, Alan Sugar, Tom Peters and Sir John Harvey-Jones.

ideas hunting

Now let's come at this search for ideas from a different route. The principle aim of *How to Generate Great Ideas* is to help improve your ability to generate ideas and so far we have concentrated on approaches you can take to generate ideas by some process or other. But other people – or places – may present you with ideas.

So I suggest you take a break from trying to think of ideas: go out and about and discover what might be sitting there waiting for you.

human beings

Go and talk to people. Obviously, if your idea will benefit your business or organization you will be talking to people within it. But consider also who else in the wider world might be a source of ideas. In business, sales people can be a particularly valuable source of information. For example, a sales person may know a great deal about what is wrong with a product – and therefore how it could be improved. It may be that it is to the sales representative that customers make their complaints. He or she also learns about the drawbacks to their product from potential customers resisting a sales pitch. And, quite likely, the sales person has valuable information about markets.

Please do not make the mistake of thinking that such information is always acted upon. Not everything in business is logical or efficient. It may be that the sales person does not feed information back to his or her employers: perhaps this person is cruising towards retirement and is not motivated to do so. Or maybe they have passed on to their employer market or product intelligence but it has not been acted upon, possibly for reasons which would not prevent you from taking up the idea.

Talk to other workers. Many employers have a suggestions box or some procedure whereby employees can put forward ideas, but many smaller employing organizations do not. So talk to the production staff, to the packers in despatch and especially talk to the service technician, who has daily to deal with problems.

If you are searching for an idea for yourself rather than within your organization for your organization, you may not be enthusiastic about approaching other people for help with ideas. In my experience many of us are hesitant about asking for help, and we often assume that we will be rebuffed, that other people will not be bothered to give us their time. But it is also my experience that this can prove to be very wrong. You may be pleasantly surprised by the readiness of other people to help you – if you take a little trouble beforehand to establish their empathy. Explain to others as far as you can what you seek to achieve and why. If they understand your motivation they may be able to identify with it.

Let us suppose, for example, that you want out of your present job and hope to break into a new career. You are looking for ideas to achieve this. You approach Alan who works in the industry. Take the trouble to explain to Alan the frustrations you feel with your present work and what you hope to get out of a career change. Frustration with our working life is something that most us have experienced at some time or another, including, perhaps, Alan, or someone that is close to him. Alan's response may be: 'I know how you feel.'

In business, do not overlook customers as a source of inspiration: perhaps your company is one that does its own market research, but perhaps not. If yours is a public sector organization, from your clients you could learn what it feels like to be on the receiving end.

Bear in mind that the customer and the user may not always be the same person: if I buy a toy for a five-year-old, I am a customer but I am not the user. From customers you can learn about their buying motives, yielding a rich source of ideas; from the user you can learn about the functioning of a product or service.

where did you buy this book?

Some recent market research concluded that around 80 per cent of the population do not regularly visit bookshops. This huge section of the population are missing out on a source of inspiration. On whatever topic you wish to generate ideas, it is almost certain that there is a book on it.

Visit one of the bigger branches of the multiple household name booksellers and you may find three or four floors, each stacked with thousands of volumes. Scroll through their computer listings and you may find, no matter how obscure the topic, there are several titles to be investigated. As with any other product, these will vary in quality, but on just about every topic or subject on which I wished to generate ideas I have managed to unearth at least one book I can work with, from which I can learn and take inspiration.

At the other end of the book retailing scale do not overlook the small backstreet bookshop and especially make the effort to see what could be waiting for you in their second-hand section. Visit a small bookshop in a sleepy market town and expect to be surprised.

Hunting for business ideas for the food industry – any titles on catering, food manufacturing and retailing – I came across, in a bookshop in a small market town in the Fens, a book devoted to unusual recipes from New Zealand. In a second small bookshop in Suffolk I came across volume after volume on food from the United States. How could I have expected to come up with that result? Puzzled by my good fortune, I enquired and discovered that we were but a few miles from a huge American airbase, which had been there since the Second World War. So I had to travel not thousands of miles but just 30 miles to find inspirational books from Kentucky, the Deep South and New England – one of which was to provide the start for a whole new product range. And continuing the hunt in a sleepy market town in rural Norfolk, I walked into a bookshop with hundreds of books on my subject: 'we specialize in them' was the totally unexpected reply to my enquiry as to whether they had any in stock.

A colleague on the lookout for ideas for the same industry remarked how lucky I had been in my find. Luck *can* play a role in your search for ideas: you could be sitting on a bus, strike up a conversation with the man sitting beside you and tell him how you are trying to come up with an idea to get Sainsbury's to stock your product: the man tells you he is Richard Branson and suggests an idea that you can see in a flash will meet your needs. You thank him and go off and the idea works beautifully. It could happen. And it would be nice if it did. But personally, I find the more I get up and go out to hunt for ideas or for the inspiration that will bring them, then the luckier I get. Make the effort rather than waiting for 'lady luck' and you put yourself in a better position to take advantage of any luck that happens to be out there.

Do not be too willing to dismiss other people or places or things as possible sources of ideas. It would have been easy for me to think that I would be wasting my time visiting a small bookshop in rural Suffolk: until I visited it I did not make the connection between it and the local American airbase. Go down routes where you and others do not readily expect to find inspiration or the idea you are looking for. Go down enough of these and you will be taking pathways that others are not taking and come up with ideas they do not come up with: you will have different ideas. And in business having something different is how you distinguish yourself from the competition and beat them.

a day at the fair

In business, you have sources of information and inspiration directed at you with which you may be familiar but not always feel you have time for. How long is it since you visited a major trade fair for your industry? Perhaps your reaction is that it is the same thing every year. Surely it can't be? Trade fairs are where others launch new products and announce improvements to existing lines: is there not something there that might give you food for thought? Is it possible that the last time you visited a business exhibition you did so in a frame of mind where you did not expect to be impressed? Are you sure then that you rooted out everything that could be of interest? Or perhaps your own company was exhibiting and you spent most of your time on the company stand.

reading time

Do you let the trade journals you subscribe to pile up and remain unopened? And when you do set aside some time to go through the backlog do you simply skim through them? Something there might strike a chord with you. Could something somebody else is doing in Vietnam or California or Germany give you a starting point in your search for inspiration?

Perhaps your business or organization isn't in the habit of paying several hundred pounds for copies of market research reports which could be of interest to you. But a summary of the report's main findings might be found in a trade journal. A pet food wholesaler has recently had his biggest success with a new product range after taking inspiration from a market survey summary revealing how consumer interest in healthy eating is widening into similar concerns over what the family dog is chomping through. So now Fido can chomp into vegetarian food, or a tasty meal with meat from animals that were not raised in factory farms, or one free of chemical additives.

Do you know what journals are currently available for your trade or have you simply been taking the same one year after year? Current journals are listed in *Willings Press Guide* and other directories.

the directory

Ahh... directories! How I have learned to value directories! It seems to me that there is always a directory: someone somewhere publishes a listing. And often I am surprised to find there are a number of directories to choose from.

In your search for inspiration, do not confine yourself to the directory that is obviously applicable. The managing director of a medium-sized communications company, seeking ideas for a mailing list he continually expands, regularly wanders into reference libraries and picks up directories at random. A directory aimed at writers included among scores of listings, names and addresses of news-gathering organizations. The thought flashed into his mind that these would be people who might have sudden need for additional communication facilities: to cover that big story which has suddenly broken, for example. This was to be the start of a mailing list that has grown into his most profitable source of new custom.

in the library

When did you last visit a library? Now a busy, thrusting go-getter like you may yawn at the thought of spending half the afternoon in a musty library. But maybe that library has a musty smell because it has old volumes in whose pages lie ideas which you can resurrect, ideas from the past that will strike everybody as new because they haven't seen them today. The new product development manager of a food manufacturer, looking for ideas for products to export to the United States, came up with a range of very traditional English recipes by leafing through pre-war and 19th-century cookery books with yellowing pages in a section of the library at the local university.

In the UK we now have around 100 universities, most of which have a business school and thus a business library: could you find the time to visit that business library? You may find it a pleasant change of environment from the bustle of the office, or something to do on a Saturday afternoon as a change from the supermarket shopping. Visit a library and you may end up starting a new career or launching a new business or emigrating.

your log book

We saw earlier in Chapter 4 how self-imposed deadlines can help focus you and motivate you. They are an example of self-discipline: another example is the self-discipline of keeping a log book of potential ideas. In your search for ideas you can make an agreement: you agree with yourself that you will start a log book and require yourself to make an agreed number of entries over a given period of time. You can help prop up your discipline by telling others what you are doing so that you will be exposed to the possibility of investigations as to how you are proceeding. Your friend Mr Negative or your colleague Ms Doubtful will be able to ask how many ideas you have in your log book.

The simplest procedure is to agree with yourself that you will make entries on a daily basis. How many entries? This in part must depend on your own realistic assessment of how difficult it will be to generate the ideas that you are seeking: set too high a figure and by failing quickly to meet your target you may become demoralized and likely to give up. Better to set a realistic target and achieve it. Better still, set a realistic target and exceed it. Certainly you should aim for an absolute minimum of one entry per day.

It is possible to make an interesting case that the number three has played a greater role in the creativity process than other numbers. It is a figure I use for a variety of purposes, so I commonly suggest a minimum of three entries per day in your log if at the outset you are uncertain as to how many you can realistically achieve. Come on, you can try to think up three ideas to put in your log book each day! A day divides neatly up into three periods of morning, afternoon and evening and you can aim to make an entry in each segment of the day. Indeed, by requiring yourself to make an entry during the morning you will help to concentrate your mind from the start of your day on the need to come up with an idea.

Take a break on Sundays and take advantage of the process we looked at in Chapter 4: stop trying to think of an entry for your log and give your subconscious time to work and you may find yourself scribbling away on Monday morning.

Take inspiration for your log from the place you are at. If you are at work, use the company's products or its systems or the activities of your colleagues to set your thoughts going. Or at home you may be able to set off a chain of thought from the comfort of your armchair: if you pick up and think hard about the contents of a catalogue or sales leaflet, does this suggest something?

Or get up and go out. On Saturday, for example, you could

go to the shops, not as a customer, but as a researcher. No doubt in business you keep an eye on what the competition is doing in your particular trade or industry but you can also take inspiration from what others in non-competing industries are doing. Are there developments in the confectionery trade that you could be taking up, or in fashion retailing?

In your visit to the shops as a researcher you are banned from taking your shopping list: you must not allow your attention to be diverted into thinking about what you need to take home for the barbecue or choosing a card for your forthcoming anniversary. Instead you must concentrate 100 per cent on what you are observing. What trends can you discern from what customers are buying? Is there anything to learn from how goods are being presented to consumers? For example, taking inspiration from a well-known chain of electrical retailers, a small pet shop now has a monthly 'event' taking place, adding interest for customers, creating the impression that there is now always something going on at People & Pets. And when that pet shop expanded into wholesaling it took with it that philosophy: there is always something going on at this wholesale warehouse, whether it's a 'summer line spectacular' or 'new product show' or 'how to beat the superstores seminar'.

can you be a bandit?

Perhaps the most obvious and quickest route to generating an idea is to take up somebody else's idea. I do not have in mind running with an idea that a colleague or someone whose help you sought has suggested for you. No, I have something else in mind here. But how to word my suggestion?

My usual approach is to ask whether you can 'adopt' somebody else's idea. I have been accused in the past of being mealy-mouthed about this: the response of the managing director of a successful company that was looking for ideas for diversification was: 'What you really mean, Barrie, is that I should consider whether or not I can nick somebody else's idea.'

A firm of solicitors I was working with to generate ideas for marketing their services put it rather well when they enquired whether or not they could 'clone' somebody else's idea.

In fact that suggestion isn't just a clever play on words: what I have in mind is the possibility that you could replicate an idea. So if, for example, your business is looking for ideas for new products and you read in the trade press that a competitor is working on a widget that will work faster because the heat will be generated from the top of the unit rather than from the bottom, can you bring out into the market-place a new product with this feature?

As you would expect, the question of whether or not you can clone somebody else's idea is alive with legal implications. Attempting to cover the legal complexities comprehensively is beyond the scope of this book and in any case I am impressed by the old saying in the legal world that the man or woman who tries to be their own lawyer has a fool for a client! But I can attempt to point out some of the legal implications that you should at least consider and perhaps pursue with your legal advisers.

The starting point is that in our free enterprise economy, once a business idea is open to the public gaze it is open to competitors to take up that idea. For example, if you are seeking an idea for a business to start and you learn of a successful small business started elsewhere offering a service collecting, ironing and returning shirts to professional people, then it seems you could adopt that business idea and set up in competition. What you could not do is to mislead customers into believing that they are dealing with the original business. The lawyers call this passing off and it is most likely to arise where your name is so similar to the name of the first business that customers would confuse the two.

So, if the idea of supplying bodycare products in simple

inexpensive packaging that helps conserve the world's resources appeals to you, you can set up in competition to Anita Roddick but it would be very inadvisable to call your business 'Body Stop'.

You will certainly need to communicate with your solicitors if you have reason to believe that the idea you wish to adopt has been given to you in confidence or the circumstances are such that you should have realized that this was so. And then, of course, parliament affords legal protection in the form of what it terms patents; broadly speaking, processes by which something is achieved. And then there is the possibility of protection in the form of a registered design.

If all this is making you think that you will have to come up with your own original idea, then I would bring your attention back to the starting point: that in a free enterprise system if an idea is in the market-place there is good reason to think that you may be able to adopt it. Bear in mind, however, that when your own idea is launched onto the market other people will also be able to take advantage of this licence in our free enterprise economy, a principle aimed at encouraging competition.

use the dreaded F word

I do of course refer here to the word 'failure'. What will be your reaction if I suggest that you should consider taking up an idea that somebody else has failed with? Perhaps it led them into bankruptcy or drove them to leap off Beachy Head. The response of Mr or Ms Negative might immediately be to dismiss it to the dustbin of failures: they will not rummage through that which they consider to be non-starters. But Mr or Ms Constructive Thinker will reason that not every idea that fails to function can have been inherently defective, especially so in business, where not everything is efficient or logical. And whatever idea has not succeeded in the past, you will have now the benefit of hindsight.

You may also have the benefit of changed conditions. In business, for example, what may have been too small a market 10 or 15 years ago may have grown into a viable market today. Changes in the market-place such as changes in consumer tastes may have given rise to new opportunities. For example, turn the clock back not so many years and four-wheel drive vehicles were sold into a comparatively small market in contrast to the mass market of the family saloon. So that bolt-on 'extra' that had been devised for four-wheel drive vehicles perhaps didn't appeal to the restricted market of farmers and others with a need to bump over rough ground. But today the market for four-wheel drive vehicles is sufficient to support three monthly magazines for the four-wheel drive devotee and hobbyist, whose reaction to that bolt-on accessory may be very different: just the thing to help personalize their pride and joy.

And new products have come onto the market-place since your predecessor tried to get the idea off the ground: that super idea for home computer users would have had an almighty struggle 15 years ago but today, with home computers a mass-market item, they support a 50-page catalogue of software, accessories and other products for the home computer user. In many homes today that computer user will be able to smile at their novelty mouse mat: 10 years ago the idea for a novelty mouse mat was dismissed: not enough offices would buy such a thing, it was said. One could not imagine solicitors rushing out to buy Wallace & Gromit mouse mats for their secretaries. But at home it makes a nice little item for that same secretary to brighten up his or her computer desk today.

In your search for ideas I say to you again, go down enough routes and you increase the chances that you will find what you are looking for. And go down enough pathways that others are not going down and you increase the chances that you will think of something different. And, especially, go down roads that others are turning away from, thanks to their negative attitudes.

brainstorming: turning up the heat

Some of the most original, inventive, practical and potentially profitable ideas I have seen generated have come from well functioning brainstorming teams. In my experience usually both quantity and quality go together: the team that churns out big numbers of ideas very commonly also gives me ideas that stand out.

A well functioning brainstorming team does not have to be composed of experienced brainstormers; nor does the team have to be one which is well established: a group of strangers can come together and within minutes we have a brainstorming team that is alive and crackling.

But practice and experience can push up both output and quality of the best teams, so maybe you should consider setting up an ongoing brainstorming team (or group of teams) in your business or organization. Perhaps they will have a specialized remit such as meeting once a month to come up with ideas for new products or to improve items in the existing product range. Or perhaps your brainstorming team will meet regularly to generate ideas in any area of activity, not just matters that manifestly need improvement or solutions to problems:

consider brainstorming ideas for those matters which are presently rumbling along OK: there is very little that cannot benefit from attempts at improvement. Your business or organization can enjoy the fruits of continuous and progressive improvement through its 'ideas team'.

If you are trying to find an idea or solve a problem for yourself, please give serious thought to getting together your own brainstorming group. Perhaps family or friends will help you. Alternatively, are you the only person that has this problem? Perhaps you already belong to an association or group among whose members you could draw together a brainstorming team. Now that the days of a job for life have gone, many if not the majority of us at some time or another will face the problem of job-hunting or enforced career change: improving your ability to generate ideas could turn out to be a priceless asset in coping with such life-changing dislocation. And by drawing upon the thinking potential of others – such as the members of a job seekers' group – and giving your own thinking the opportunity to spark off them, you will broaden your range of potential ideas.

So if you need to come up with fund-raising ideas for your animal rescue society or you and other villagers need to come up with ideas for your campaign against the expansion of the airport, then form an ideas team.

booster techniques

Alongside practice, boost the productivity and output value of your ideas team with 'booster techniques' (BT). Introduce one or more of the following when you sense the team is beginning to lose its sparkle: don't wait for it to become stale or grind to a halt. Look out for tell-tale signs such as the team member casually looking at his or her watch or long, leisurely yawns.

BT1: twin scribes

A lively team, especially a bigger one of six or eight members, may come up with this technique themselves if they are in competition with another team.

The team organizer appoints *two* scribes to write down the ideas generated, dividing the team into two halves, each with its own scribe. Halfway through, the two scribes can swap team members. This is in effect creating mini teams within teams and then changing the composition within the mini team, maximizing the opportunity for individual to interact with individual, at a risk of some duplication of ideas.

BT2: musical chairs

Being seated in a brainstorming session that has gone on for some time can result in body stiffness or give rise to a sense of lazy comfort. An inactive body may help create the conditions for the brain to slow down. Every so often, such as at the end of each competition between the teams, each team should stand up and the members move round the table to the next chair. Taking this one stage further, part of the session can be conducted with the members of the team standing.

Movement of the body does seem to encourage movement of the mind. With one energetic group I had worked with for some time we experimented with requiring the members of the team to move round the table each time an idea was suggested. Once each team member had gone round the table and was back at their original seat, we went into reverse: each idea saw the team members moving one seat at a time round the table the other way. This procedure was introduced at the end of quite a long session when the team members were tired and also getting somewhat jaded and it was a way of injecting both some energy and some humour into the proceedings.

BT3: inspiration from within the four walls

If the team start to run dry, invite each team member in turn to stand up, leave their place and discover what inspiration they can draw from within the room. If time is short or the team is a big one, ask two members to try this. Reading matter may be a resource: for example, there may be newspapers or journals or other written material to hand, which may or may not be related to the subject matter of the brainstorm. If the text picked up seemingly has no connection with the subject matter to hand, the team member will have to work harder to take inspiration and their thoughts will have to range wider.

Use objects within the room as a starting point for thoughts that you or the others would not otherwise perhaps have had. Touch the object: does its shape or texture give you a thought? What about the colour? Supposing you pick up at random one object and place it together with another – is there something forming in your mind now?

BT4: play with the words

I have used this technique both at the end of a long brainstorming session and when the brainstormers have had several meetings.

Look at your list of ideas: take a word from one idea and marry it to a word from another idea. For example, in a warmup exercise one team included among the uses of a brick: 'catch snails in the garden', idea number 37. We ran our eyes down to idea number 61: 'chock for caravan wheel'. Circle a word from each idea, put them together and see if that starts you off in a new direction. So here we circled the word 'in' from number 37 and the word 'caravan' from number 61 to give us 'in caravan'. So we asked ourselves to what uses could we put a brick inside a caravan? This produced another nine ideas within the space of some 90 seconds, including using the brick to prop open the door, and using the brick as a device for gaining entry when we arrived on holiday and realized we had left the key to the caravan at home.

BT5: silent brainstorming

Many of the techniques we have looked at to help boost output involve movement or sound. Injecting a change of approach can be beneficial since both silence and inaction may stimulate the brain in a different way.

Invite the brainstormers to reflect in silence. Give them a period of time (I have found three minutes to be useful) during which they do not speak but continue their thinking, writing down the ideas that come to mind. At the end of the allotted time each member in turn reports back his or her ideas to the other members of the team.

This can work surprisingly well as a break from the usual hurly-burly of brainstorming, but it works better for some individuals than others. If this silent brainstorming has been productive, consider having a second and longer session of, say, up to 15 minutes. Alternatively, if your brainstorming team is big enough, you can pull out the two or three members for whom this has worked best and send them off to work on their own in silence, while the remainder of the team carries on brainstorming in the usual fashion. At the end of this experiment bring all the members of the team back to report on and merge their ideas.

BT6: sequence brainstorming

Silent brainstorming is a tactic for putting pressure on the individual, since at the end of the period of silence he or she will have to report back on the fruits of his or her own thinking labour. Sequence brainstorming gives us another means of applying a little bit of pressure to the individual team member, but the pressure is more obvious and some team members may be disinclined to this approach.

Brainstorming in the usual way allows members of the team to function at their own pace and throw in ideas at random. Where the team goes into a sequence session we go round the team and each member is required in turn to contribute an idea. How much pressure you want to exert here must depend to a considerable extent on the personality of the team members: a degree of pressure is already felt by each member as he or she awaits his or her turn. As each person's turn comes, he or she will have to 'pass' if they have nothing to contribute: the tension can be moved up a notch or two if the team organizer keeps tabs on the number of passes and announces the person's running total on each occasion that he or she passes.

Almost nail-biting tension can be achieved by combining sequence brainstorming with silent brainstorming: the member who has no idea to throw into the pot when it comes to his or her turn is allowed a period of silent grace while the other team members wait to see if their colleague can yet come up with an idea. This does put the individual on the spot: one minute of silence in this circumstance can seem a long time.

BT7: surprise them

Where you have divided your group into teams competing against one another, make each team organizer stand up and report back the team's achievements to the entire group. On each occasion ask the team organizer to remind us of the team's name and to pronounce the team's achievements in a loud clear voice.

Always try to find something encouraging to say about the results – unless it is clear to all present that the team has simply not made the effort or has not taken the exercise seriously. As the session goes on and output and quality improve, the point will come at which it is clear a team has done well: recognize this, declare it to be so – and then tell them they can do even better and unexpectedly give them another few minutes, asking them to improve on even the great result they have achieved so far.

This can be particularly effective with the final brainstorm of a session. Announce beforehand that it is to be the last brainstorm of the day and ask everybody to make a special effort. When they have done this and sweated through a final grand effort, then ask them to sweat yet one last drop of blood: give them the final, final time extension.

At the end of a long tiring day, this is likely to be met with groans, in which case you can draw the sting out of it with a red herring. When the brainstormers sit there relaxing under the misconception that they have finished, I remind them of the power of three, how the number 3 has a special role to play in the creative process. I then put this question to them: 'What would be your reaction if I were to ask you to continue brainstorming for a further three hours?' The uproar with which tired brainstormers greet this indicates a lack of appeal in the proposition. When you, as MC at your brainstorming session, suggest to your brainstormers that they go on into the dark hours, you may, depending upon your status with them and the degree of authority you enjoy, have to dodge and duck missiles thrown at you.

Then offer a compromise: ask them to give you a tiny fraction of that time, one final burst to beat all that has gone before. The group usually acquiesce mildly to this in relief of having been let off the prospect of a further three hours of mental workout...

let's pretend

Many of the approaches and techniques we consider in *How to Generate Great Ideas* are practical in nature: hands-on stuff, get-up-and-go-out suggestions, such as tracking down other people who may be able to suggest ideas to you, or uncovering other people's ideas that you may be able to clone. And you have tools and tactics to stimulate your thinking: a whole toolbox full of them in the next chapter.

But it is also possible, of course, to use highly creative means to produce ideas, perhaps even literally to dream them up... The common thread running throughout the approaches we will look at now is an element of pretence.

crystal ball gazing

I don't know what will be the purpose of the idea you are searching for, or what is the problem you are seeking to solve, but it may be that one of the approaches you could take is the highly original one of crystal ball gazing.

For this exercise, there comes free with this book an imaginary crystal ball. While your eyes were diverted reading the previous chapter I placed the crystal ball in front of you. Can you see it? You may be able to bring your search for an idea to a conclusion by gazing hard into the crystal ball.

Let us suppose, for example, that you are seeking ideas for a new product to launch into your trade or industry. Gaze into the crystal ball and see into the future. What changes are going to take place in the future? You can see these changes in your imaginary crystal ball. Perhaps they are changes brought about by new technology. How far into the future can you see? Five years, 10 years, 20 years? What benefits will these changes bring to customers and users? As you gaze into your crystal ball you are viewing benefits that customers will have in the future which they do not enjoy in the present.

Having witnessed in your imagination customers and users enjoying benefits they do not have now, switch back into a highly practical mode. To what extent can you give customers that missing benefit with means that are open to you today? Can you somehow or other give them 10 per cent of the benefit, or 20 per cent or 50 per cent? There's your new product.

try this

Where you ask yourself to change suddenly the direction of your thinking drastically, to switch from highly creative mode into a practical hands-on mode of thinking, it may help you to accompany this change in the direction of your thinking with a change in the direction of your body. Switching from one mode of thinking to another, I stand up, move a distance of at least a few yards and recommence thinking while facing a different direction.

non-existent problems

What is going to be your reaction if in your search for an idea I ask you to expend your labour and time on trying to find a solution to a problem that does not exist? I appreciate that your first reaction may be that this is a peculiar suggestion and you may be inclined to skip the next page or so; or your reaction may be that you have quite enough real problems on your plate now that you have to solve without spending valuable time in trying to solve problems that don't exist.

But we *are* trying to solve your real problem, although by taking a route that most other people will not be taking. For example, at a seminar devoted to job-seeking ideas for redundant managers and professionals, one of the participants, aged in his 50s, had spent nearly two years trying to secure employment in his particular field. He had a specialized technical qualification obtained in his younger days which had been a financial and academic struggle for him to acquire. The session had produced some ideas but he faced the difficulty that there had, in recent years, been a surge in the number of new entrants to the profession, without a corresponding increase in need for their services.

I suggested to Len, who had become increasingly despondent in the months before he joined our seminar, that he pretended he had this problem: I asked him to imagine that he was unemployed but without any qualifications. Overcoming initial scepticism, Len found that the more he applied himself to this problem, the more his thinking opened up. Reviewing the options open to him as an unemployed man in his 50s with no qualifications he found nothing that appealed to him at his local job centre or situations vacant column. Presented with this problem, Len realized that in seeking to find a job as an unqualified person there were no real openings that appealed to him in any measure. So what could he do? His conclusion was that in these circumstances he would consider setting up his own business.

So his solution to his imaginary problem was for him the radical idea of breaking away from a lifetime of being employed to become his own boss.

Having worked through to a possible solution to the imaginary problem, we then of course switched back to the actual problem we have to face up to: can we learn anything from the process we have gone through with our imaginary problem? In particular, are there any lessons to be learnt from the solutions we have come to? Indeed, can we apply the same solution to this problem?

Where this approach can be most helpful is when our thinking has got stuck in one channel: every time Len looked at his CV, what stood out for him above everything else was his qualification, together with the professional experience he had acquired in consequence of holding that qualification: seemingly, it had never occurred to Len to ignore this.

Len launched his small business drawing on a hobby interest he had held for many years. Today, he employs two people, one part-time, one full-time, both recruited from the dole queue, and both of whom Len persuaded to have a go at some income-producing activity that was unlike anything else they had done before.

This approach of endeavouring to solve problems that don't exist is commonly found in new product development. It can be used both to come up with ideas to improve products and for new products.

A natural way of thinking in product development is to take an existing item and seek to improve it by overcoming its existing defects or shortcomings. The more creative approach is to dream up a problem and pretend the product is saddled with it. What will you do to cure this problem?

Let us suppose, for example, you are trying to come up with ideas for a new line in toothpaste. When you launch a new product on the market-place, your task is to induce in customers the feeling that you have something unlike anything they have seen before.

What if the tube of toothpaste sometimes leaks before the customer gets it home from the supermarket? What would you do to solve that problem? Perhaps you would change the composition of the toothpaste so that it did not ooze from the tube, or perhaps you would produce something with a more solid consistency. Perhaps you would come up with a completely different type of container that would not leak. Possibly this container could serve also a second function, maybe one connected with the use of toothpaste or maybe one used for a different purpose in the bathroom? Or one for kids that has a fun function after its life as a toothpaste container has finished?

While most other people are trying to solve real-life problems, when you spend some of your time trying to come up with solutions to problems that do not exist, you open up the possibility that you will be going down roads that others are not following and may, as we have seen before, come up with ideas that other people do not arrive at.

wishful thinking

Using 'wishful thinking' as a means of generating ideas can be both productive and a pleasurable interlude: you conjure up your wishes.

Len's team at our seminar on job-seeking ideas included Rachel, seeking to return to work after a 15-year absence devoted to bringing up children. Having been out of the work scene for this period of time, Rachel admitted to, and demonstrated, a lack of confidence. This led her to have low aspirations for herself. We asked her: if you could do anything, what job would you like to have? Her natural response was that she couldn't see the point in thinking about such things, she had to concentrate on the reality of her situation, her lack of experience and lack of qualifications. But we had to prise open her thinking.

When we finally persuaded Rachel to think hard as to what she would *really* like to do if she could do anything at all, the next question was: if you were 16 years old, what career would you like to pursue? This question required an even bigger leap in her imaginative thinking but caused her to open up her mind to even wider possibilities. Ultimately, she pursued none of the possibilities envisaged by her wishful thinking but she was left with this valuable result: having lifted her eyes up off the ground to look at the sky she did now set higher goals than her early low aspirations and came up with the idea for a new career she was able to launch upon after only 12 months at college.

a gigantic leap in your thinking

Most 'new' products launched onto the market are not revolutionary, unlike anything else that has gone before; the majority of new products are modifications of that which exists already, but modified to such a degree that what the customers see strikes them as new. But push the technique of wishful thinking to its limits and you may come up with some product or innovation that really is something new.

Pushing wishful thinking to its outer limits, what if there were no restrictions or limitations or constraints *at all* on what you could do? Using the technique of visualization we looked at in Chapter 4, picture yourself doing *anything*. Sit back in your chair, take slow, deep breaths: for you, for the next two minutes, you can do anything, you can be anything, you can go anywhere you please. What will you do?

This is a challenging exercise – but if you can really do it, you may come up with a real prize. It requires you to make the most enormous leap in your thinking: since the day you were born, since you first opened your eyes, your whole existence has been subject to limitations: scientific limitations, physical limitations, financial limitations. But for you, shortly, in the picture you create in your mind, there will be *no* limitations. You can do *anything*. Will you go back in time and be a Roman charioteer? Will you be a butterfly? Will you be 1,000 feet tall? Let your thoughts and imagination roam as freely and as widely as possible.

Having settled on what it is you will do and where you will go, dim the lights and go there, and stay there for two minutes. What a fantastic experience!

At the end of the two minutes switch out of this free-flowing, highly creative mode of thinking back into a boiler-suit mode of thinking. Ask yourself why you wanted to do this thing. What benefit would you get from it?

Persuade others to join you in this enjoyable experience: when they reveal their daydreams and what it is they want from them, they will be revealing information which may be gold-dust: for what we are seeking to bring out here are deep-seated, probably long-desired benefits denied to the people.

Having unearthed this deep-rooted desire, as with the crystal ball gazing, you now ask yourself how far, subject to real-world limitations, you can give the person the benefit they yearn for. Can you by existing means give them 5 per cent of what their daydream would do for them? Or 10 per cent or 20 per cent? If so, there you have another new product.

face masks

If wishful thinking can be a pleasurable experience, 'face masks' can be a *fun* way to bring a new slant to your thinking. It can be a way to generate ideas different in character from that which your personality normally predisposes you to.

A useful time to try this approach is when you feel your own creativity is winding down: at that point you then imagine you are someone else. Imagine yourself in the shoes of another person whom you consider to be a creative thinker and apply *their* mind to your ideas generating session. You can, if you apply yourself hard to this role, have some of the benefits of that person's mind without them being present.

This other person can be anyone at all – real or fictional: what matters is your belief in their creative thinking skills. I have had suggested over the years an assortment of characters: as you would expect, entrepreneurs such as Richard Branson, and business gurus such as Sir John Harvey-Jones; political figures from Margaret Thatcher to President Roosevelt; and creative geniuses from the world of entertainment, such as Steven Spielberg from today and Walt Disney from yesteryear. But the list also includes John, 'my boss', and Pat, 'my mum'.

Props may help you think yourself into the role, although their use will probably require a little planning. 'Sherlock Holmes' brandished his pipe; 'Margaret Thatcher' borrowed a handbag; and 'Richard Branson' played with his model aircraft. Abandon yourself, apply someone else's mind and benefit from their creativity.

your ideas toolbox

Commonly when you set about a task, tools will be available for your use. Wire a three-pin plug and you will use a screwdriver; type a letter and you can use a typewriter or a PC.

Hire a professional painter to decorate your lounge and he or she will make use of tools along with professional techniques to save time and make a better job of it: he or she will paint the door from the top, working downwards, so that if the paint runs it won't spoil what has already been painted.

So too with ideas generation: you can use tools and professional techniques to save effort and do a good job.

morphology strips

Ideas generation even by your own effort need not consist solely of concentrated thinking. You can use scissors and strips of paper to generate ideas.

Take a sheet of A4 paper, or better still, a sheet of thin card, and cut it up into strips, each about an inch deep and the width of the A4 paper. This is a simplified form of an approach often used to devise new or improved products, the starting point being the attributes of the existing product. In this simplified form it works both for product development and coming up with ideas or solutions to problems in other fields. It is used by writers, for example, to come up with ideas for storylines.

Let us suppose you are a scriptwriter on that vintage, oft-repeated television situation comedy 'Dad's Army'. You have joined the writing team shortly before production ceases: the programme has run for many series and storylines are getting hard to come by. But you do not have to spend hours staring at a blank sheet of paper waiting for inspiration. A professional approach would be to generate ideas utilizing morphology strips.

On our first strip of paper we would write the names of, say, five leading characters. On our second strip we would write five 'doing' words. Our third strip is for objects, our fourth strip for places, in both cases ones we associate with the Home Guard and its members. Finally, we have a fifth strip of paper on which we write down types of characters we might expect to meet in a storyline involving the Home Guard.

1.	Captain Mainwaring	Cpl Jones	Pike	Walker	Godfrey
2.	discovers	wants	falls	guards	moves
3.	whistle	rifle	boot	bomb	bell
4.	hall	church	trench	field	beach
5.	ambulanceman	wife	land girl	vicar	colonel

The more strips you use, the more you open up the possibilities, moving from attributes possessed by your subject-matter to attributes it *could* have. So in this example, strip number four could be extended to two strips, one, as now, comprising places immediately associated with the Home Guard unit and its members, and a further strip comprising places one could conceivably associate with them, such as a railway station or a shop. Still more could the possibilities be opened up by expanding strip number four into three strips, this time having also a strip for places one would *not* associate with the Home Guard or its members, such as a brothel or the Antarctic.

You can expand the number of strips once you have exhausted the possibilities with your existing morphology strips, but you may be surprised how many combinations are thrown up by moving about even four or five strips each containing four or five words.

Lay out the strips in front of you and begin by reading down each column to see what that gives you. Reading down column one gives us:

Captain Mainwaring
discovers
whistle
hall
Ambulanceman

The first storyline suggested here then seems to be that Captain Mainwaring discovers a whistle in the church hall and then calls an ambulanceman. Or perhaps he discovers a whistle which belongs to an ambulanceman. This doesn't strike me as very promising. So we move strip number two sideways to the left, thus bringing the second word in line beneath the first word of strip number one. We have:

Captain Mainwaring
wants
whistle
hall
Ambulanceman

This gives us as the start to our storyline: Captain Mainwaring wants to whistle, which does not sound a very strong storyline; on the other hand, this is a comedy that we are writing. Move strip number three along one word and we have:

Captain Mainwaring
wants
rifle
hall
Ambulanceman

We now have as the start of our storyline: Captain Mainwaring wants a rifle. We know that Captain Mainwaring already has a rifle so perhaps for some reason or other he wants a new one. Or perhaps – now that our thoughts are set in motion – Captain Mainwaring wants to *practise* with his rifle. Why should he wish to practise? Perhaps the unit is to take part in a competition or in a field exercise. Perhaps Captain Mainwaring believes another member of the unit, a subordinate, is a better shot than he. This sounds promising. Once we have a start our creativity kicks in.

Where does he want to practise? We need somewhere that will give us some laughs: back to the morphology strips. Strip number four suggests he practises at the church hall, which seems uninspiring, but move the strip along one word and we have the possibility that Captain Mainwaring practises shooting with his rifle at the church.

Once again, thanks to the morphology strips the creative juices are flowing and I am not staring blankly into space: perhaps Captain Mainwaring practises inside the church in the belief that the building will muffle the sound and he will not be discovered secretly practising. Or perhaps he practises behind the church in the mistaken belief that no service is taking place inside.

We seem already to have a possible storyline taking shape, a storyline which is the product of a combination of mechanical process and inspiration that has come in consequence of that process. We can move these strips this way and that way and alter the order in which we read them to produce hundreds of possibilities. Moving strip two along one more and strip number four to the top, for example, would give us as a possible storyline: at church Captain Mainwaring falls... falls into? falls in love? falls over? If the latter, why would this happen? These are more interesting questions to aid creativity and keep the ideas flowing.

mind mapping

A roll of wallpaper can be an extremely useful piece of equipment for use in the process of ideas generation. It need not be a current design: an end of range or oddment will suffice. It can help you bring out ideas that might otherwise remain undiscovered.

Most people are introduced at school to the concept of mind mapping, although it may not have been called that – a member of the older generation is likely to refer to a mind map as a spidergram. Mind mapping is a method of flinging out your thoughts with minimal interruption.

If you haven't met mind mapping before, pick up a pen and take an A4 sheet of paper. In the centre of the sheet of paper write down the subject around which you wish to generate ideas. If we return to our example of creative writing, let us suppose that your first script for 'Dad's Army' was so well received you have been invited to write a second.

In the centre of your sheet of paper write the words 'Dad's Army'. Now, moving out from the centre, write down anything that comes to mind that is associated with the subject matter. This could be incidents – people – places – concepts – whatever. Leave a space between each. Keep writing. Keep writing.

When you have covered the paper, draw breath, then pick up a pen or pencil and draw a coloured line between two of your recorded thoughts which have a connection. Use a different colour for the next connected pair, another colour for the third pair and so on.

From my mind map I picked out as my first pair 'warden' and 'duty'. Could this give me the start of an idea? Is the warden on duty when something happens to him? I then picked out 'butcher's van' and 'special constable' – I always associate the police with motoring. Does this give me the germ of an idea? Is the constable investigating the theft of Corporal Jones' van? This would leave the unit without its transport – what unsuitable alternatives might they be forced to use?

can you draw?

Many are the variations on how you go about mind mapping. Try out different approaches to find what works for you.

One small change that may set your mind thinking along different routes is this: rather than writing down the subject around which you wish to generate ideas, make a simple drawing in the centre of the sheet of paper to represent the subject. For example, when working with a manufacturer who was looking for ideas for new products for dogs, at our first attempt at mind mapping we wrote the word 'dog' in the centre of the sheet of paper. For our second effort we attempted a simple drawing of a dog. As this produced some different thoughts we were then encouraged to try our hand at drawing an example of large breed, choosing an alsatian as our symbol. This produced some different thoughts which encouraged us to have a fourth session working with a symbolic drawing of what was supposed to be a tiny dog, a chihuahua, but which with my drawing skills looked like a mouse; this produced one or two bizarre thoughts, so a colleague with better drawing skills than mine produced a passable likeness of the miniature breed.

programmed mind mapping

For your first attempt at mind mapping fling out your thoughts in a totally random fashion on the paper, without working to a pattern or categorizing them.

An alternative approach is to pursue a line of thought until it is exhausted, and then return to the centre and work on another train of thought. When you run out of steam with that come back to the centre again to start on another line of thought, and so on.

This more orderly approach to mind mapping, sometimes referred to as programmed mind mapping, still benefits from an element of randomness but can encourage you to be more exhaustive in your search by pursuing a line of thought rigorously. This approach is also easier if you are accustomed to working with lists, which is a very orderly way of recording material. Quite likely you have been making lists of the ideas you have generated thus far.

But lists have dangers for the creative thinker. Most likely you have written your list in a vertical column: be aware that there is a tendency for us to subconsciously regard items at the top of the list as having greater importance. There is also a temptation to discard items because they do not sit well in the list; they do not seem to fit. And with a long list it is not so easy to make a connection between items towards the top and items towards the bottom. So listing your ideas and thoughts as you produce them can mean you are subconsciously applying a brake to your creativity.

forced connections

Mind mapping is a technique that explores thought association. But once your mind map is complete, one of the uses to which you can put it in an attempt to come up with highly original ideas is to go against the grain and abandon the use of association.

Once you have exhausted the process of associating two or more thoughts with which you can see a connection, do not lay your pen down like other people. Select one of your recorded thoughts and then pick another which seems to have no connection.

Then work hard to try and come up with a connection. Probably in the great majority of instances you will not be able to think of anything viable and to do so will be much harder work. But if you persevere, then once again you will be taking an approach that most other people are not taking and thereby increasing the chances that you will come up with something different.

the pain barrier

It is late at night. You are tired. You've been working on your mind map since early evening. You've exhausted it. You know you can now sit back: you've done the job. You've taken it as far as you can go. You can't come up with any more ideas or thoughts or starting points.

I would say to you: now go back to it. Make a superhuman effort. Keep going where other people would have packed up. Force yourself to come up with more ideas. Dig deeper. Go through the pain barrier. You *can* come up with more ideas. There is still something there that you can unearth.

You may have a pleasant surprise waiting for you: go through the pain barrier, go down, through, beyond where you thought you could go. Dig deeper, and in so doing not only will you make the discovery that, yes, there is more to be mined but you will find also the deeper you go the more original and unusual the ideas you force yourself to bring forth. Go through the pain barrier and you may find the very best.

the wallpaper technique

When you have covered the piece of paper with your mind-map you will be tempted to think that you have finished. The size of the sheet of paper you use to record your mind map can exert a limiting influence: while you still have paper to cover you are more likely to push on. So at the very least purchase sheets of

A3 paper. Better still, buy a wad of flip-chart paper, a sheet of which is several times the size of A4.

And best of all? Visit your local DIY store and purchase a roll of wallpaper. In the oddments bin you will find end-of-range rolls or discontinued lines. Place your roll of wallpaper on the floor and unroll a few metres with the unprinted side facing upwards. Now you have room for the world's biggest mind-map. You can work on it every day. Who knows what you will come up with?

analogy

When we draw an analogy we compare like with like. Drawing an analogy can be particularly fruitful in helping you to generate an idea to solve a problem and is often used by product development people to think of ideas both for improving products and for new products.

A simple use of the technique is to take an improvement that has been made to a product or service and apply that improvement to other – including totally unrelated – products or services.

In solving problems an analogy is frequently drawn with nature: the problem solver, having examined his or her problem, then considers the solution evolved by nature to a similar problem. While working in an ideas session with engineers employed by an aircraft manufacturer, I learnt that when jumbo jets were first conceived as an economic form of air travel, much thought was given to how such huge aircraft could get into the air with a minimum extension of existing runways. From humankind's earliest attempts to fly we have learnt from birds. Most large birds fly from water or jump from cliffs using thermal air currents to become airborne but the stork is a large bird that flies up from the ground. In their search for the most efficient wing design; jumbo jet designers took into account how the stork lifts from the ground.

So if, say, you find yourself searching for an idea to solve a design problem that causes your product to move on slippery conditions, you could consider how a seal manages to haul itself out of an icehole onto slippery ice. Or if you find yourself looking for ideas to improve how your widget can move across a rocking surface, look to see how animals cope with shifting sands. You will often find that nature has evolved an idea millions of years before human beings.

small solutions

When faced with a 'big problem', very likely you will think only of the 'big solution'. But consider as an alternative having not one solution but a number of small solutions.

These piecemeal solutions may not add up to a complete resolution of your problem but perhaps you cannot come up with the one big idea or perhaps it is not feasible to carry it out: that big solution may, for example, require the expenditure of big bucks.

The best illustration I have come across is from the grand but ageing hotel that also had ageing lifts which moved more slowly than some of the ancient staff. The elderly staff had other characteristics to recommend them, but the slow lifts did not. The unloved lifts were the biggest source of complaint in the visitors' comment book. The solution was new lifts, the estimate was out of this world and out of the question. No solution?

The constructive thinker doesn't give up here: he or she now comes at the problem from a different angle. What is it that irritates guests to cause them to complain? It must be the waiting for the lift to arrive and its slow progress thereafter. Waiting equals boredom. If we can afford to install a new lift it would go faster and cut down the waiting time and thus the boredom. Instead, can we not reduce the boredom by appearing to reduce the waiting time? Let us give the guests something useful to occupy their time.

Full-length mirrors were installed either side of the lift doors to enable guests to check on their appearance while waiting for the lift to arrive. Inside the lift the walls were covered on one side with a useful location map for visitors and on the other side helpful information about nearby facilities. None of this made the lifts function any faster but at a cost of a few dollars the number of complaints about the lift dropped drastically.

your hero

In your ideas toolbox, among your collection of tools, techniques and aids you could keep a photo.

Most likely your objective for generating an idea or ideas is part of a bigger plan or undertaking. Perhaps you are trying to come up with an idea for a new service to offer as part of growing your small business into a nationwide enterprise. Or maybe you are coming up with an idea to overcome a problem you have encountered in developing a revolutionary new widget that is going to take the world by storm.

Of course, others before you have struggled and made a success: you can learn from them and in particular you can learn from them how they came up with their ideas. So if you come across articles in newspapers or magazines about others who have succeeded in your field, don't turn the page, read them and see if you can find inspiration. Has this person published an autobiography you could study? Does an unofficial biography give you some insight into how they came up with ideas?

As a writer, I learnt from my favourite author of nonfiction books. In an interview with a writer's journal he was asked how, when faced with a blank sheet of paper, he got inspiration for his ideas. My hero replied that he just started writing, especially if he didn't feel like it, and once he got warmed up the ideas began to come.

I cut out the article, with its accompanying photo of this highly successful writer, and pinned it to the wall above my desk. So now at 9.00 am on a wintry Monday morning if I do not feel like writing and do not feel the inspiration coming, I put pen to paper and begin to write. And my hero was right...

is it any good?

Is this the idea that you were looking for? How much time and effort you put into weighing up your ideas must depend on the importance of the idea to you, whether you are looking for something that will keep the kids out of your way for the day or whether you are looking for something that will change your life.

If you are seeking the big idea, a framework for your thinking through which you work for each idea, will help you give each of the ideas a chance to survive. Going through an evaluation procedure will help avoid the temptation of too easily dismissing an idea which at first sight seems perhaps too outrageous or too implausible, until and unless you pause to consider.

Much of my ideas generation experience has been with people trying to generate an idea that would dramatically affect their lives: trying to come up with an idea for a business they could start, that would perhaps get them out of the job they hated and felt trapped in, or would get them off the dole and redundancy behind them, or would give them the income they needed.

That is an example of just the sort of idea where an evaluation process should include seeking the advice of others, discovering the views of those with greater or specialized knowledge or experience in the matter. Of course, where your advisers include professionals such as accountants or lawyers, they are more likely to be concerned with the feasibility aspects of your idea rather than, say, whether you will find personal satisfaction in carrying it out.

I have found the evaluation process falls into three stages, the first of which takes us back to the beginning of the book and the beginning of the search for an idea.

what are your goals?

How does this idea fit in with your goals? What was it you were seeking to get out of the idea? For example, with would-be entrepreneurs seeking ideas for a business I ask them to list what they want from their business idea: what should the idea be capable of delivering? Naturally individuals have their own lists but some oft-met aspirations include an idea:

▧ with sufficient potential;
▧ to enable me to pay off the mortgage;
▧ that will enable me to create something to hand on to my children;
▧ that will give me some personal satisfaction: I want to feel I am doing something and achieving something that is worthwhile;
▧ that will enable me to use my creativity, which in my humdrum job is under-utilized;
▧ that will let me spend my days doing something I enjoy so I never have to experience that 'Monday morning' feeling again;
▧ that will present me with a challenge.

Drawing up a list such as this gives you some criteria to measure your idea against.

Sometimes you need to generate an idea over and over again, such as an idea for something to keep the children occupied for a day during the school holidays; in such a case you may have objectives which you have to satisfy every time you need to come up with an idea, but you may also have particular objectives on particular occasions; it is easy to concentrate on the latter and lose sight of your standard objectives. So it may be that today you need an idea that will keep the children away from the house while the painters are working and there is wet paint for the children and the dog to get all over themselves: but do not forget your ever-present objectives in trying to find an idea for something to occupy the children, such as, that, in this day and age, they will remain safe.

how feasible is it?

Will the idea work? Before the kids start jumping up and down with excitement at your idea for getting them to clear that favourite beauty spot of litter in return for allowing them to have a pet rabbit, you need to consider what they will do for lunch and whether you have time to do them a packed lunch and whether you have anything in the house that they would eat for a packed lunch and who will pick them up at the end of the day as you have promised Aunt Cecilia you will visit her in hospital?

For the big idea, you need to set down a checklist you can work through for each of the ideas. In our example of an idea to start a business, most people's checklist includes the following:

- ▓ How difficult will it be to find or carry out reliable market research?
- ▓ How difficult will it be to finance?
- ▓ How difficult will it be to 'produce' the product or service?

■ How difficult will it be to acquire suitable premises?
■ Would we need a licence to operate?
■ How difficult would it be to obtain it?
■ How difficult will it be to carry out the sales function?
■ How difficult will it be to maintain quality?

These questions are illustrations of five aspects you can use as springboards for devising a checklist:

■ evidence that the idea will work;
■ money;
■ ability to carry out the idea (assets, skills);
■ law;
■ the future.

some techniques

For both phase one and phase two of your evaluation process you can make use of techniques to help you more fully and more accurately evaluate the idea.

The obvious approach most people take is to list advantages and disadvantages of their idea. You can simply take each of the factors you need to consider from your checklist, apply each to your idea and make two lists: a list of advantages and a list of disadvantages. One list may be considerably longer than the other, thus seemingly giving a clear picture of how matters stand. But this simple method of evaluation does not give relative weight to each advantage or disadvantage: we need to consider, of course, not just how many points there are in favour of the idea or against it, but how much each of these matters.

weighting

A clearer picture than the simple lists give us can emerge if we take each advantage and disadvantage in turn and allocate it a weighting. The weighting can be expressed numerically: at one end of the scale award 1 for a minor disadvantage; at the other end award 3 for a major disadvantage; and award 2 for one falling in-between. Repeat the process for the advantages. Add up the respective totals and you may find this gives a somewhat different result from the simple list.

A third perspective can be obtained if you add up and consider how many advantages and disadvantages have been awarded a '3' rating. You may find, for example, that although the advantages have a higher overall score than their opponents the disadvantages, very few of the former have major worth, whereas there lurk in the disadvantages' side several heavy-weights: how would you feel about lots of small and not-so-small advantages against a few major drawbacks?

another use for a mind map

You could now go on to make use of a mind map, since mind mapping can be used both to generate and evaluate ideas.

This can be a 'mopping up' exercise: because of the free-flowing nature of mind mapping you are likely to pick up some pros and cons otherwise missed. Also include how you might deal with or minimize problems and this will help you to get them into perspective. And include how you might maximize opportunities and the best use of strengths.

At the end of this you may be left with a firm impression one way or the other as to the overall merit of your idea.

Beware of these factors working against valid evaluation of your idea:

■ Pressure of time, eg 'He'll go mad if I haven't come up with the right idea by then.' Is this really true or is it over-dramatization? Giving insufficient time to the evaluation process will not help you come up with the *right* idea.

■ Ambition, eg 'If I could just come up with the right idea and pull this off somehow, it will change everything.' Would it really change everything or is there again an element of over-dramatization? Are you being realistic about what you can achieve in the light of assets and time frame?

■ Over-reliance on data: figures can easily convey a false impression. And over-reliance on forecasting, such as future sales figures based on past sales figures, can seduce you into being too optimistic.

the human factor

You analyse and consider and consult and research and this all points you one way – but what if that is not the way you feel you want to go? What if, having done all the things you should do, the conclusion is to go ahead, but your reaction is: 'I don't want to but I don't know why I don't.' Or vice versa. People describe their doubts in different ways. Some people will say: 'I've got this sixth sense'. Others might say: 'I can't pin it down, but my instincts are...' More commonly, I've heard it said: 'I've got this gut feeling...'

Your intuition is not to go the same way as the conclusions of your analysis. Is it alright for you to disagree and head off in the opposite direction to that which the process of analysis points? A desire to trust your 'gut reaction' or 'sixth sense' is an example of how the evaluation process is affected by the circumstance that you are a human being. So too will you be affected by personal preference – 'It's my favourite colour' – and emotion: 'But I like her.'

Research in the United States has concluded that when we rely on our intuition we are in fact drawing on accumulated experience which has been retained by our subconscious. Support for the proposition that this is the process at work comes from experiments demonstrating that as we get older our instincts about what is the right decision to make are increasingly likely to give us the correct answer. This is because as we get older we go through, and our subconscious logs, a greater number of experiences from which we are able to learn.

So, perhaps it is true that the older you get the wiser you become – and thus the more comfortable you can feel in relying on your instincts as to whether or not you have had a good idea.

My experience of helping thousands of others to evaluate their ideas has brought home these lessons:

■ Very few ideas are perfect. As with other aspects of your life, you will have to live with some drawbacks to your idea.
■ Do not dwell disproportionately on the drawbacks: you must give due weight to the strengths of your idea as well as to its drawbacks.
■ Many apparent drawbacks can be overcome – with your enhanced ability to generate ideas.

But you will not be able to apply these lessons unless you have the vital ingredient we looked at in Chapter 2, an element of such importance we cannot leave the subject of generating ideas without returning to it in our final chapter.

successful thinking

Having worked with thousands of people endeavouring to generate ideas I am often asked who is best at coming up with ideas. Are women better than men, I am asked. Or this question is quite often put to me: do young people lack the experience to come up with ideas or does it get more difficult as you get older and set in your way of thinking?

The last two or three decades have seen heightening of interest in how the brain works and in thinking skills. Much has been written about the different functions of the left side and the right side of the brain, and in particular how the right side of the brain provides our more creative thinking.

During this time business people especially have shown an awareness of what is called lateral thinking and have benefited from the writings of that towering figure Professor Edward de Bono. The lateral thinker is a person who deliberately searches for alternative ways of looking at things or of doing things and I now see a lot of people making the conscious effort to cultivate this way of thinking.

Many of us who are middle-aged and over have become aware of how in our schooldays we were drilled in 'vertical' or logical thinking. We were taught to criticize, evaluate and rationalize; we were encouraged to use our imagination or creative thinking abilities only in art and for English essays.

Children are taught differently today – or so I am told – but the majority of adults over 40 probably had this type of learning experience at school, years of learning which did not allow our lateral thinking skills to flourish as they might.

We wouldn't survive very long in the world without logical thinking skills but most of us find such thinking easy thanks to lots of practice whereas our lateral thinking skills have often been neglected and are rusty. Lateral thinking can help you turn up the ideas, then logical thinking can help you sort and develop them.

As we have seen, research concludes that pictures are less restrictive on our thinking than words or language, so use your visualization skills to switch from one mode of thinking to another. For logical thinking, picture yourself standing outside a garden gate looking at a straight path to a front door. The door is your goal and once you have opened the gate and begun your progress you keep to the straight line of the path without deviation until you reach the door.

The essence of lateral thinking can, I think, be conveyed by a trampoline: bouncing ideas around. So to put your mind into lateral thinking mode, picture yourself beside that trampoline, catching the ideas as they bounce off.

From the many people I have worked with who are seeking to generate ideas, if I were asked to put together a composite picture of that person most likely to win gold, for certain we would see in them characteristics of the lateral thinker. These, contrasted with the approach of the vertical thinker, are:

lateral thinker	vertical thinker
goes 'cross country'	sticks to the path
explores that which is unlikely	follows the most likely

In vertical or logical thinking mode you are sorting and selecting, closing off lines of thinking. In vertical thinking mode you are looking to bring out why something won't work; in lateral thinking mode you are trying to see what can be made of it. And it is there that the positive thinker finds his or her task much easier. We must return again to the important issue we looked at in Chapter 2, that of your attitude.

perseverance

Alarm bells start ringing in my head when I hear: 'Well, I suppose I might as well give it a try.'

Positive thinkers display determination. They keep trying to generate the right idea. And if they've come up with something less than perfect they try to make it work.

But set out on your quest for an idea with a half-hearted attitude and you are likely to give up too easily. And such an attitude stems from insufficient motivation, you are not hungry enough for it. Which brings us back to the need to be clear as to what you want from your idea. What do you *really* want?

If you are being made to generate ideas as part of your job and you can't see the point, then I can't see you generating great ideas. Perhaps you need to work hard and concentrate on the positive reasons there are for generating the idea – or put up a fight.

If you are generating an idea for yourself and you are not sufficiently motivated, you must ask why not. I have to tell you that a worrying proportion of people I have worked with who are attempting to come up with a life-changing idea had never found time to find out what they really wanted to do.

If you are half-motivated you will be too ready to find comforting excuses and early reasons why you won't succeed.

optimism

More alarm bells ring in my head when I hear: 'We're having a terrible day, we might as well pack it in and go and watch the cricket.'

A badge of the negative thinker is the ready assumption of failure. If you are great at generating great ideas you are almost certainly not a pessimist.

In asking you to be optimistic, I am not asking you to be jumping up and down: you don't have to give me the 'ra, ra, ra' type of false optimism. Let us be optimistic soundly based upon our experience, advice we have taken, research we have carried out – and move on. It might be the next approach that works for you, it might be the next tool that you take out of your ideas toolbox that makes your thoughts begin to spin and some interesting ideas appear.

The person I have worked with who was the worst at coming up with ideas told me: 'I never have any luck…'

A reminder: everything in the world achieved by humankind begins with an idea, so improve your ability to generate ideas and you improve your ability to do anything. And you can improve your ability to generate ideas dramatically by developing a positive attitude, which in turn will help you to be a lateral thinker.

But to generate lots of ideas, of which some will be great ideas, there is one more asset you need.

the unspoken factor

In writing this book my function has been not so much that of a tutor or a teacher but a reporter: I have reported back to you on what I have seen work for thousands of others and on the lessons I have learnt in working with and helping them to generate ideas – in some cases ideas that will revolutionize their life.

Sadly, I found that many people I have worked with have lacked confidence in their ability, including their ability to come up with worthwhile ideas. I recall in particular, Gerry, who, persuaded by his wife and friends, had enrolled on my seminar to come up with ideas for a business he could launch. Gerry crept up to me before we started and said in a lowered voice, 'I don't know if I should be here today. I'm not any good at thinking up ideas.'

You and I have together been through the approaches and techniques that I have seen work for others: this I did with Gerry. After our seminar he wrote to me: 'I didn't think I would be able to come up with any ideas, yet I have thought of very many.' Gerry hugely under-estimated what he was capable of.

What has raised its head here is something that at least one half of the population hardly ever discusses: our level of self-confidence. This is not something that most males want to talk about. It's not a subject men talk about at the pub. 'Real men' might ask their friends over a drink how they rated the team last night but they are unlikely to ask: 'What about your levels of self-confidence, John? How's your self-confidence doing?'

Yet those who come up with plenty of ideas and lots of gems are confident that they can do so.

I do not know the reasons for it, but I can say that *most* people coming to me for help to generate the idea they seek under-estimate what they are capable of doing.

And what is the point of coming up with great ideas if you do not carry out any of them? Many of the people I have worked with to come up with ideas under-estimate both their ability to do so and their ability to put that idea into practice and make a success of it. A sociology professor tells me it's not just the folk I meet who want to generate ideas: he claims the majority of people play down their own abilities and he blames it on our education system. But of course, lack of confidence in the ability to generate ideas, and to follow them through, is something other readers may suffer from – we are not here talking about *you*. Are we? However, just in case, before commencing your search for an idea, remind yourself:

■ of some of your achievements to date;
■ of some of your skills and abilities;
■ that you have the benefit of the tools and approaches and techniques and lessons from *How to Generate Great Ideas*;

then – go and do it!